P—
Use this book to
strengthe your inner
life that God might
do His work in I
thru you.
Pray for me each
day you use this guide

Thanks,
Eddie
4/23/90

The Christian Companion

About the Compiler:

Elizabeth Rundle lives in Cornwall where she works as a school secretary. She is a keen contributor to local religious radio programmes, and has written for a variety of Christian magazines. She is also a methodist lay preacher.

The Christian Companion

Compiled by
Elizabeth Rundle

Marshall Pickering

Marshall Morgan and Scott
Marshall Pickering
3 Beggarwood Lane, Basingstoke, Hants RG23 7LP, UK

First published in 1987 by Marshall Morgan and Scott
Publications Ltd
Part of the Marshall Pickering Holdings Group
A subsidiary of the Zondervan Corporation

ISBN: 0 551 01357 5   Paperback
ISBN: 0 551 01495 4   Hardback

Text set in 10/11 Sabon by PRG Graphics Ltd
Printed in Great Britain by Anchor Brendon Ltd, Tiptree, Essex

With thanks to my husband Wilfred for his help with my dreadful spelling and checking my mistakes – without his love and support this could not have been written.

1st January

He who was seated on the throne said, 'Behold, I
am making all things new.'

Revelation 21:5

I step into the first day of this new year like a child making the first
footprints on a snow-covered path. New beginnings are fun,
challenging, exhilarating. Help me Lord, to learn from the mistakes and disappointments of last year. The slate is clean now and
everything is new – new opportunities, new experiences to colour
my life. True, the former things have passed away and nothing
that has happened in the past can be altered. So now, Lord, let me
be born again to enthusiasm and hope, committing my life into
the hands of Jesus who was with me yesterday (last year) is with
me today (this new year) and will be with me through all time to
come.

New mercies each returning day hover around me while I pray;
New perils past, new sins forgiven,
New thoughts of God, new hopes of heaven.

John Keble

2nd January

Commit to the Lord whatever you do.

Proverbs 16:3

At this time of year people are awash with New Year Resolutions;
more often than not, fine sounding resolutions are doomed to
failure. I should like to make my resolution for this year to be to
commit whatever I do to my Lord. Even in the smallest things,
when I'm tempted to cut corners, to take the easy way out, let
things slide . . . Lord, you were a carpenter, skilled and precise
work which left no room for slapdash – as I commit my small life
and smaller works to you, show me the value of a job well done.

Teach me my God and King, in all things Thee to see,
And what I do in anything, to do it as for Thee.

George Herbert

3rd January

'Lord,' Martha said to Jesus, 'If you had been there . . .'.

John 11:21

Both Mary and Martha spoke to Jesus in a way which shows plainly they felt that everything would have been different if He'd been there. Just like us today, it's almost an accusation against God, or at best, it's a way of excusing ourselves . . . it would have been different, Lord, if you had been there. The vital truth is that Jesus *is* with us – He has promised to be with us always, there is no room for the half-hearted 'if only . . . .' Lord, help me to be positive, not to daydream about what might have been – help me to live knowing Your presence all the time.

Open our eyes Lord, we want to see Jesus . . .
To reach out and touch Him . . . and say that we love Him;
Open our ears Lord, And help us to listen . . .
Open our eyes, Lord, we want to see Jesus.

Robert Cure

4th January

Martha asked 'Lord, don't you care that my sister has left me to do the work by myself? Tell her to help me.'

Luke 11:40

Feeling hard done-by is not uncommon. In any organisation from churches to play-groups, Young Farmers to Women's Institute, there are those who do the bulk of the work and the coasting majority who very often moan the loudest. Preserve me Lord from the trap of self-righteousness; self-inflicted labourings to create the impression so similar to the Pharisees who Jesus condemned. Help me get my life into perspective . . . I am not the only person who is busy, and perhaps my very 'busyness' has clouded out the joy of receiving an honoured guest.

My every weak, though good design,
O'errule, or change, as seems Thee meet.
Jesus, let all my work by Thine,
Thy work, O Lord, is all complete.

Charles Wesley

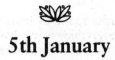

5th January

The desert shall rejoice and bloom as the rose.

Isaiah 35:1

When I look outside my window it certainly seems a long, long way to go before the roses begin to blossom, but even now, in the depths of winter, I know that time will come. Forgive me, Lord, that when I look ahead, things seem so remote and I lose heart. Why is it that looking back, the time has gone so fast, yet to try to look ahead the time threatens to drag, if not stop altogether? Today, Lord, I'm going to be bright and optimistic. I may even buy a bunch of flowers to cheer the home and remind myself of my Creator's perfect timing.

Sweet Rose of Sharon, blooming for me,
Jesus it is the emblem of Thee,
Beautiful flower, fairest that grows,
I'm glad that I found Thee, sweet Sharon's Rose.

Staff Captain Gay
Salvation Army

6th January

The first thing Andrew did was to find his brother
and tell him, 'We have seen the Messiah.'

John 1:41

When we are bursting with good news it's natural to rush out and tell our friends . . . no girl would turn up at the office and say nothing of her engagement nor would any fisherman slink into the pub and not mention a prize-winning catch. No, we've got to tell. I can imagine Andrew dashing off to find his brother with his good news, news that was not only going to change their lives but change the whole world. Good news is for sharing – have you got some good news to share today?

> God's spirit is in my heart,
> He has called me and set me apart:
> This is what I have to do –
> Go tell everyone
> The news of the Kingdom of God has come.
>
> Alan T. Dale

7th January

Lord, I do believe – help my unbelief.

Mark 9:24

Funny how I believe without a murmur all the secular wonders like communication satellites, micro-surgery – even the telephone. I have no idea how they all work, but I gladly accept that they do. I believe in God, but then most people in the world believe in God, one way or another. Forgive me Lord that I so easily forget You: in so many problems I come to You as a last resort; somehow my limited mind cannot conceive Your almighty power . . . I need so much help with the grey areas of my understanding: give me the grace to realise I can't understand everything, but Lord, I do believe, help my unbelief.

> Just as I am, though tossed about
> with many a conflict, many a doubt,
> Fighting and fears within – without,
> O Lamb of God, I come.
>
> Just as I am, Thou wilt receive,
> wilt welcome, pardon, cleanse, relieve;
> Because Thy promise I believe
> O Lamb of God, I come.
>
> Charlotte Elliott

8th January

Give thanks to him and praise his name. For the
Lord is good and his love endures for ever, his
faithfulness continues through all generations.

Psalm 100:4, 5

The book of Psalms covers every human emotion from despair to
elation; they mean so much because no matter what happens,
there is the recurring declaration of God's unfailing love. When I
stand back to look at my life, I see how God has guided me – thank
you, Lord, that when I couldn't see how things would work out,
You never left me . . . I fuss and fret but my Saviour has given me
strength for each day.

> *Great is Thy faithfulness,*
> *Morning by morning new mercies I see,*
> *All I have need Thy hand has provided,*
> *Great is Thy faithfulness, Lord, unto me.*

Thomas O. Chisholm

9th January

Lord, when did we see you hungry, feed you, or
thirsty and give you something to drink? When did
we see you a stranger and invite you in, or needing
clothing and clothe you . . . ?

Matthew 25:38

We can all sit comfortably reading the words of Jesus and filling
our heads with high ideals, but when it comes to actually putting
ourselves out to invite a stranger home, visit the sick, continue to
send money for the hungry . . . well, that's something else. The
Pharisees were shocked by the thought of such involvement, they
wanted to be holy without coming into direct contact with
people's real needs. Sometimes, Lord, I have to admit that's how I
feel, too. I have no excuses . . . Your words tell me that whatever
we do for the least and lowliest of mankind, we do it for You.

Faith is a gift of God. Without it there would be no life. And our work, to be faithful and to be all for God, has to be built on faith. Faith in Christ who said, 'I was hungry, I was naked, I was sick and I was homeless and you did that to me.' On these words of His, all our work is based.

Mother Teresa of Calcutta

10th January

Greater love has no one than this, that one lay down his life for his friends.

John 15:13

January 10th, 1858 was a bitterly cold night and a young woman of twenty sat in a minister's study gazing at a picture of Jesus hanging on the cross. She was so moved by it, she scribbled some verses hastily on a piece of paper, but, on second thoughts, she felt they were so inadequate she screwed them up and threw them in the fire grate. Later, she changed her mind, retrieved the charred poem and showed it to her father. Rev. Havergal composed a tune for his daughter's haunting words, though to many, the words stand as a devotion by themselves. As I read these words, Lord, I ask myself, what have I done for You, or anybody else today?

Thy life was given for me
Thy blood O Lord was shed that I might ransomed be,
And quickened from the dead.
Thy life was given for me,
What have I given for Thee?

Frances Ridley Havergal

11th January

. . . in the place, O Lord, you made for your dwelling the sanctuary, O Lord your hands established.

Exodus 15:17

Sanctuaries, places of worship, God's House, call them what you will, they've been built in every land and every century – even this moment, somewhere a church is being built. These places where our parents were buried, or we were married, christened, worshipped for many years, they do have special meaning for us. When I walk into a great cathedral its very solidity hushes me to reverence – yet God is as much in a cathedral as in a Friends' Meeting house; He is to be met in the hospital chapel or on the street corner with the Salvation Army band. William Bullock helped to build the first church for the settlers in Newfoundland, he was their minister and wrote the words below for the very first service there. Dear Lord, guide me in the way I can help to build up my part of the church, Your family, with the bricks and mortar of kindness and sincerity.

> *We love the place O God*
> *Wherein Thine honour dwells;*
> *The joy of Thine abode all earthly joy excels.*
>
> William Bullock

12th January

Gideon said: 'if the Lord is with us, why has all this
happened to us?'

Judges 6:13

We witness quite the most appalling accidents involving innocent, friendly and caring people. Floods, aeroplane crashes, motorway pile-ups, earthquakes, bombings and so on . . . children, old people, mothers, anybody and everybody catapulted in seconds from normality to disaster. How often has mankind turned on God with an anguished *Why*? Lord, life seems so unfair at times – but I suppose it is pointless to ask questions this side of Heaven. I don't understand; I just hold on to my faith that Your love will use every situation for good.

> *God is love:*
> *And he redeems us in the Christ we crucify:*
> *This is God's eternal answer*
> *To the world's eternal Why.*
>
> Fred Pratt Green

13th January

'Do not be afraid . . . for I am with you, and no-one
is going to attack and harm you, because I have
many people in this city.'   *Acts 18:9*

Time after time the Bible tells of situations where people thought
they were all alone, the only ones left, all the world against them,
and for every such story we read how wrong they were! Corinth
was a cosmopolitan city with all the vices, delights and degra-
dation of any modern city; and just like any bustling hub of
activity it could be a very lonely place. O Lord, may Your encouragement to Paul be mine today – help me look on this city
knowing that there are many who worship You, and on these arid
streets full of hurrying strangers, I will remember You are with me
and I won't be afraid.

> *O Master from the mountainside*
> *Make haste to heal these hearts of pain:*
> *Among these restless throngs abide,*
> *O tread the city's streets again.*

Frank Mason North

14th January

Have you entered the storehouse of the snow?
                                            Job 38:22

How children long for the snow – what fun skiers have whistling
down the ski-slopes – how ethereal the postcards and photographs of snow; but how hazardous for the elderly, the disabled
and the weary commuters. The microscope tells me about the
storehouse of the snow and I am speechless before a Creator who
can enable each separate snowflake to have its own unique in-
dividuality. Yet, here in an anonymous flake is mirrored the
human family in its infinite variety: and if I can accept that, then
who am I to argue with Eternal Wisdom? I trust what my eyes see,
Lord help me to believe that no matter how I have behaved or
what I have done, the saving love of Jesus can forgive.

Though your sins be of scarlet, they shall be white as snow.

Isaiah 1:18

15th January

If anyone has material possessions and sees his
brother in need, but has no pity on him, how can
the love of God be in him?

1 John 3:17

The story of Henri Dunant, the founder of the Red Cross Society
is both touching and challenging. His harrowing experiences of
tending wounded and dying soldiers, compelled him to declare
'all men are brothers'. Tragically today, somewhere in the world,
men will be at war, both men and women will be indoctrinating
children with racial hatred. Lord I pray for the hearts that are so
full of hate, even the young hearts, I pray for those today who will
be wounded and lie waiting for help, or death. Thank You for all
the work of the Red Cross throughout the world and may I spend
my life in constructive peace.

O brother man, fold to thy heart thy brother,
Where pity dwells the peace of God is there.

John Greenleaf Whittier

16th January

For I am convinced that neither death nor life . . .
nor anything else in all creation, will be able to
separate us from the love of God in Christ Jesus.

Romans 8:38

It took the death of a friend for me to grasp the meaning of the
phrase 'love is stronger than death'. Through my tears I knew that
I still loved her even though I could no longer see her, speak with
her or hear her gentle laughter. Death in one sense deprives us but
at the same time our feelings do not alter overnight. The experience brought me to see that once love has been given it can't be
snapped like an electricity cable – real love continues across
thousands of miles, across the span of a life-time and not even
death can defeat it. So then, Lord, if that is the strength of human
love, I know that nothing in all the world can separate me from
Your love; my love is frail – Your love is eternal.

Jesus my Lord will love me for ever,
From Him no power of evil can sever;
He gave His life to ransom my soul
  Now I belong to Him.
  Now I belong to Jesus
  Jesus belongs to me;
Not for the years of time alone – but for eternity.

Norman J. Clayton

17th January

. . . David would take his harp and play, then relief
would come to Saul, he would feel better.

1 Samuel 16:23

What a vast, colourful and international language we have in music. When we consider that there are only eight notes in the octave, the permutations are astounding. Something for everyone to enjoy from Gregorian chant to country and western, from Chopin to bagpipes. Thank You Lord that I can have so much music, right in my kitchen with the radio, or cassettes in the car; thank You for the memory of concerts, for the way music can change my mood and also for the way I can lift my voice to praise Your Holy Name.

'Nothing elevates the soul (of the believer) nor gives it wings, nor liberates it from earthly things, as much as a divine chant.'

St. John Chrysostom

18th January

There is one body and one Spirit . . . one Lord, one
Faith, one Baptism, one God and Father of all . . .

Ephesians 4:4

As a small child I remember being seriously puzzled over all the different denominations – Anglican, Methodist, Salvation Army,

Roman Catholic, Quakers, Congregationalists, Baptists, the list is endless . . . and I certainly had no idea of all the cults, sects and other world religions. As communications shrink the world, as we learn more, and care more for other colours, races and cultures, may we become more aware of the fundamental brotherhood of all mankind. Lord God, Father of us all, help the world grow closer – help me to make friends.

> *What shall our greeting be,*
> *Sign of our unity?*
> *Jesus is Lord.*
> *May we no more defend barriers He died to end;*
> *Give me your hand my friend,*
>   *One Church, One Lord.*

Fred Pratt Green

19th January

> Again I looked and saw all the oppression that was taking place under the sun: I saw the tears of the oppressed – and they had no comforter . . . .

Ecclesiastes 4:1

Today I offer prayers for the growing band of skilled people who take their knowledge, expertise and experience to countries of the developing world . . . nurses, doctors, teachers, agriculturists, builders, engineers, pilots and technicians. Their work may be scratching at the surface but they are there, where they are needed, giving material and spiritual comfort because of their living faith in Jesus. Lord, You have no hands but ours – thank You for willing, sharing hands and minds, and for the comfort of caring hearts.

> *And be Thou known when fears transcend*
> *By Thy best name of Comforter.*

Alfred Vine

20th January

Don't have anything to do with foolish arguments,
because you know how they produce quarrels
2 Timothy 2:23

Haven't we all had arguments where, when the heat of the moment has passed, we wonder 'what was all that about?' Petty, foolish, unnecessary bickering with unending repercussions. Quarrels in the morning can spoil the entire day, they split clubs, even churches. Other people's arguments are always hot-headed and trivial but our disagreements are always justified . . . or so we try to tell ourselves. O Lord, help me to hold my tongue when I feel waspish, give me a tolerant heart and guide me through this day without being pig-headed and foolish.

> *Perverse and foolish oft I strayed,*
> *But yet in love He sought me,*
> *And on His shoulders gently laid*
> *And home, rejoicing, brought me.*

H. W. Baker

21st January

Moses said: 'O Lord, please send someone else to
do it'
Exodus 4:13

I know people in hospital who would like a visit, I know a mother who would appreciate some baby-sitting, there are elderly on whom I could pop in and do some shopping or little odd job. The play-group is short-handed and Meals-on-Wheels could do with another driver . . . I know one hundred and one circumstances where a helping hand is needed. Forgive me Lord for my 'Moses syndrome', the way I sit back and wait for someone else to act: if it is Your will, show me how to serve in my neighbourhood.

> *Then I heard the voice of the Lord saying:-*
> *'Whom shall I send? and who will go for us?'*
> *And I said, 'Here am I . . . send me.'*

Isaiah 6:8

22nd January

No longer will a man teach his neighbour, or a man
his brother saying 'Know the Lord' because they
will all know me from the least to the greatest.

Jeremiah 31:34

The religious leaders in Biblical times liked to distance themselves
from the ordinary people, enjoying, as it were, keeping God for
themselves. Therefore Jeremiah's teaching was quite outrageous.
Over the centuries since the days of Jesus, time and again, religious leaders have sought to foster this separation, telling the
people what to do, making them feel inferior and unworthy. Yet is
it just for the inferior and unworthy that Jesus lives today . . . to
be known personally by any who ask him into their lives. Lord, I
am totally unworthy, but I dare to approach the cross, believing
You are willing to live in my heart.

My God, I know, I feel Thee mine . . .
I hold Thee with a trembling hand
But will not let Thee go:
Till steadfastly, by faith I stand,
And all Thy goodness know.

Charles Wesley

23rd January

Are not five sparrows sold for two pennies, yet not
one of them is forgotten by God.

Luke 12:6

Little sparrows at the bird table, alongside starlings, blue-tits,
blackbirds and robins – just a few little birds . . . I wonder how
many sparrows there are in the world? How many birds of
varying species? Millions . . . and every feather on every wing is
perfectly designed. O Lord, if You are responsible for these birds,
then surely, I must believe that You care for me too. When I feel
forgotten, when I'm fearful for tomorrow, show me the chirpy
little sparrows . . . and I will remember the words of Jesus.

Beneath His heaven there's room for all
He gives to all their meat
He sees the meanest sparrow fall
Unnoticed in the street.

Edward J. Brailsford

24th January

Jesus said 'Then neither do I condemn you. Go now
and leave your life of sin'.

John 8:11

I can just imagine the crowd with the Pharisees coming to Jesus
with the woman whom they had caught 'in the very act' of
adultery. (The man is conspicuous by his absence . . .) Jesus
could have lectured, moralised, scolded . . . but all he did was to
quietly invite anyone in the crowd who was perfect to throw the
first stone. Nobody is perfect; they knew it and we know it too.
Lord, when I'm ready to criticise, condemn, gossip and generally
blacken other people, help me to stop and remember my own sin.

Long my imprisoned body lay
Fast bound in sin and nature's night
My chains fell off, my heart was free,
I rose, went forth and followed Thee:
No condemnation now I dread,
Jesus, and all in Him is mine.

Charles Wesley

25th January

Jesus said: 'Haven't you read this scripture? "The
stone the builders rejected has become the capstone
(cornerstone)" '

Mark 12:10

One of the definitions in the dictionary for cornerstone is indispensible part. There's a great deal said about foundation stones,

but not so much about the cornerstones of buildings. If I think of Jesus Christ as the cornerstone of my life, the indispensible part of my day, I can see the significance of the body of believers combining to build a spiritual house – each stone has a part to play, whether it is at the bottom, unseen or unsung, or whether it is in full view. O Lord, if I have any sharp edges which make it impossible for me to 'fit in', then with maturity of faith, in coming humbly to learn of you, break away all those edges which hinder Your Gospel.

> *Christ is our Cornerstone*
> *On Him alone we build.*
> anonymous tr. J. Chandler

26th January

> These are they who have come out of the great tribulation, they have washed their robes and made them white in the blood of the Lamb . . . never again will they hunger, never again will they thirst . . . and God will wipe every tear from their eyes.
>
> *Revelations 7:10*

Whatever the world holds for us it is a comfort to know that one day, in God's time, suffering will be at an end. When I think of the brave men and women who hold fast to their faith despite persecution, even physical torture, I recall these words from Revelations. Trials of this life will be washed away in the blood of Jesus who took the whole of life's sufferings, cruelty and sin at Calvary. The innocent millions who, because of political ineptitude and downright greed, lie hungry and thirsty across the world . . . one day, thank God, they too will know the peace of His Kingdom. Lord, today my prayers are for the people under great stress and trial, some for political reasons, some for very personal reasons, but their tears fall as one.

> *All my trials, Lord . . . soon be over.*
> Negro spiritual

27th January

... 'Love your neighbour as yourself ...'

Matthew 19:19

It's OK giving a helping hand to the neighbours when you get on well with each other – it's easy when you know it's only now and then, and anyway, they'd do the same for you. But Jesus made it crystal clear that a neighbour was in fact anybody who needs a hand. Forgive me, Lord, that I want to qualify my care and give it only when and if it suits me; teach me to love in that broad, compassionate sense that just gets on with the act of caring without fuss or obligation. A German theologian wrote to his niece, 'nothing matters like caring.' Lord, show me my neighbour.

When I needed a neighbour, were you there, were you there?
And the creed and the colour and the name don't matter,
Were you there? Were you there?

Negro spiritual

28th January

And He took the children in His arms, put His
hands on them and blessed them.

Mark 10:16

Children! Exasperating little hot-heads – dependent, loving little cherubs – noisy, untidy mixtures of prying eyes, grazed knees and ever-open mouths ... the product of our Love ... the hope for the future. Jesus gave children a special place; he stopped whatever He was doing and gathered them around Himself, and blessed them. He made the adult listeners uncomfortably aware that they had lost the trust and enthusiasm they had once known as children. Yes, all too often, it's through contact with children that we realise how cynical we have become. Lord, I pray your continued blessing on the children I know, and for a reawakening of my own sense of wonder.

I think when I read that sweet story of old,
When Jesus was here among men,
How He called little children as lambs to His fold
I should like to have been with them then . . .
I wish that His hands had been placed on my head,
That His arms had been thrown around me
And that I might have seen His kind look when He said,
'Let the little ones come unto me!'

Jemima Luke

29th January

. . . a time to be silent and a time to speak . . .

Ecclesiastes 3:7

In the prayer of a 14th century nun it says these words:– 'Lord, keep me from the habit of thinking I must say something on every subject, on every occasion.' How that needs to be my prayer today! On the phone, in the fruit shop, at the hairdresser . . . it doesn't matter where, a constant stream of my ill-informed 'wisdom' flows freely. Lord, teach me the wisdom to hold my tongue, lest because of all my noise, I fail to hear your Spirit speaking.

Master speak, and make me ready
When Thy voice is truly heard:
I am listening, Lord, for Thee,
Master speak, O speak to me.

Frances Ridley Havergal

30th January

I lie awake: I have become like a bird alone on a
housetop . . .

Psalm 102:7

There is nothing more lonely than to lie awake watching the clock through the leaden hours of night. Each minute drags endlessly on into the unfriendly blackness. But I'm not really alone . . . right now there are heaps of people feeling just the same. The Psalmist knew what it was like being lonely, feeling cut-off from friendship and support and Jesus, in those startling seconds on the cross cried out His feeling that God had abandoned Him. Alone! Most merciful and loving heavenly Father, help me to reach out of my spiritual darkness, touch me with your presence, enfold me, support me, and give me sleep tonight.

Jesus protects, my fears be gone!

Safe in Thine arms I lay me down,
He smooths my bed and gives me sleep.

Charles Wesley

31st January

Have mercy on me O God; wash away my iniquity
and cleanse me from my sin.

Psalm 51:2

Forgive me Lord, this hasn't been a good day. I've sinned in thoughts, words and deeds . . . I've been a rotten example, and I feel miserable that so many good intentions have gone down the drain. Just like the Psalmist, I cry out for cleansing too, even though this is the end of the week, fill me with the assurance that I can start again, now, in this moment, I can put the past behind me. Lord, please give me Your strength for the rest of this day.

Almighty God, to whom all hearts are open, all desires known, and from whom no secrets are hid; cleanse the thoughts of our hearts by the inspiration of Your Holy Spirit, that we may perfectly love you, and worthily magnify Your Holy Name; through Jesus Christ our Lord, Amen.

1st February

Where there is no vision, the people perish (revised
version)
Proverbs, 29:18

This is a low time of year, Lord; pretty hard to have any sort of
vision. It's still wintry outside, my heart feels a bit frost-bitten
too . . . I feel empty. I can understand how some lose their faith in
these spiritual doldrums – Father, in these quiet moments, grant
me a vision of the spring – grant me a vision of the rich blessing to
be reaped when christians wake-up and glimpse the vision of
Jesus. Yet these blessings are not automatic bonuses dropped
from above . . . they have to be sought, longed for, earned,
worked for together and shared with one another in love.

> *Be Thou my vision, O Lord of my heart*
> . . . .
> *Be Thou my best thought in the day or the night*
> *Both waking and sleeping, Thy presence my Light.*

8th century Irish
versified by Eleanor Hull

2nd February

Jesus wept.
John 11:35

One of the most revealing verses in the Bible. Jesus must have been
very fond of and close to Lazarus – he showed that there is no
virtue in pretending to be unemotional, Jesus wasn't too proud to
show how much he cared, nor did he hide the fact that death is an
overwhelmingly sad occasion for loved ones left behind. Lord, in
times of death and distress, don't let me be ashamed of the tears I
can't control, but give me the assurance that for my loved one,
death is a new beginning into a sphere I cannot understand, but I
have faith that it is the beginning of eternal joy with Jesus Himself.

In Christ we live
In Christ we sleep
In Christ we wake and rise,
And the sad tears death makes us weep
He wipes from all our eyes.

John S. B. Monsell

3rd February

'I tell you, open your eyes and look at the fields'

John 4:35

I always get caught out with that popular party game where a tray of everyday items is on view for 15 seconds, then covered up while everyone tries to write down what was on it. Hardly anyone gets the list complete. I look but I obviously don't always notice. Lord, open my eyes to people around me, help me to be aware of their burdens and worries, give me the insight to feel when I can be of use without interfering. Show me what I can do in the fields of my experience, open my heart as well as my eyes.

I heard the voice of Jesus say:
'Look unto me, thy morning shall rise
And all thy day be bright'
I looked to Jesus . . . and I found in Him my Star, my Sun

Horatius Bonar

4th February

Do not be terrified: do not be discouraged for the
Lord your God will be with you wherever you go.

Joshua 1:9

Joyce Grenfell told the story of a little boy who, when asked what he thought God was, replied 'God's not a "think", He's a "feel" '. We can be too intellectual about God, trying to reason and prove His presence with us, when in reality God is truly 'a feel' – when we are anxious, terrified even, by the implications of illness or the results of drug or alcohol abuse, when we are discouraged or lonely, it only takes the sigh of a prayer, the honest admission of failure and need of God, and we shall have that inner 'feeling' of His strength. Lord, I go into this day knowing you are with me every moment.

> *Wherever He may guide me*
> *No want shall turn me back;*
> *My Shepherd is beside me and nothing shall I lack.*
> *His wisdom ever waketh, His sight is never dim,*
> *He knows the way He taketh*
> > *And I will walk with Him.*

Anna Laetitia Waring

5th February

> Peter turned and saw the disciple whom Jesus loved
> was following them. When Peter saw him, he asked
> 'Lord, what about him?' Jesus answered, 'What is
> it to you – you must follow me.'

John 21:20

I'm convinced that in the inmost heart of all of us there is a raging busy-body! However much we have on our plate there is always time to stop and stare at someone else and wonder what they are doing, why and how. The disciple Peter was, reassuringly, no different. And in his answer to Peter, I believe Jesus speaks to us today words which plainly mean 'mind your own business – get on and make sure you are doing what is right . . . ' Lord, I know I'm guilty of looking over my shoulder to see what others are doing – help me to live my own life following you.

> *Follow, follow . . . I will follow Jesus*
> *Anywhere, everywhere . . . I will follow on –*
> *Follow, follow, I will follow Jesus*
> *Anywhere He leads me I will follow on.*

W. O. Cushing

6th February

'If anyone would come after me, he must deny himself and take up his cross and follow me'.

Mark 8:34

I'm thinking today of a young man called Andrew who has left his parents comfortable farm and gone to Africa; he has learnt a tribal dialect and works with christian nationals teaching them about compost, about different varieties of crops and the general best use of land and resources. He is but one of thousands of christians who, feel the call to become actively involved in helping others yet by doing so, they have to deny themselves what we take for granted – family meals, evenings out with friends, a warm bed, shops full of choice, television entertainment. Thank you Lord for these dedicated lives – challenge me that I am content to do so little; I offer my prayers of support and gratitude for all those who today are bearing a cross for Your name's sake.

Each new-born soldier of the Crucified
Bears on his brow the seal of Him who died.
    Lift high the Cross
The love of Christ proclaim till all the world adore His sacred
    Name.

M. R. Newbolt

7th February

The Lord gave, and the Lord has taken away; may the name of the Lord be praised.

Job 1:21

Lord, I'm so concerned for the families facing up to the death of a baby or little child . . . our society is not geared to cope with bereavement of tiny lives which seems the more poignant because of the preceding happy months of excited planning for a new arrival. All the buying and preparation for the baby, the hopes and jokes about its future – then suddenly there is only numbed bewilderment, devastating grief. The old testament character Job lost his family, his herds and his health yet his story deals with the way in which he never blamed God, even though he was at the end of his tether. He knew that there is nothing in this world that we can control, possess or call 'ours'. Our own lives are a priceless gift and the lives entrusted to our care are also treasures to love, cherish but not to stipulate the length of their days. Heavenly Father, be a mother's strength through loss.

. . . this is another needy area for prayer. Thankfully modern science has eliminated many more still births, but the whole question of medical ethics is heartsearching and the fact is that fewer perinatal deaths mean that parents feel even more alone . . .

Maureen Long

❧

8th February

Encourage one another daily, as long as it is called Today, so that none of you may be hardened by sin's deceitfulness.

Hebrews 3:13

This verse reminds us again how important it is to gather together and to build each other up in faith. Sin's deceitfulness readily tells us that we don't need to go to church, we are just as good as so and so, or it doesn't matter if we miss now and again . . . our hearts are not so wonderful that they cannot slowly become hardened into apathy. So today, Lord, may I encourage those in the family, those amongst whom I work and worship, help me to keep to the discipline of prayer for friends who face an uphill struggle today; and may we all by our prayers encourage our priests, ministers, pastoral workers, Sunday school teachers, social workers and stewards of Your flock.

Remove this hardness from my heart
This unbelief remove:
To me the rest of faith impart,
The Sabbath of Thy love.

Charles Wesley

9th February

Bear with each other and forgive whatever griev-
ances you may have against one another. Forgive as
the Lord forgave you.

Colossians 3:13

It doesn't seem to matter who or where we are, we are bugged by clashes of personality – at school, shop, office, in the choir, at the Bible study . . . everything would be alright if only 'thingame' wasn't there. Perhaps I should ask myself do people feel that way about me? Can I be off-putting, irritating, argumentative and generally Dicky Opposite? O to see ourselves as others see us. Lord, I ask for tolerance, help me to bear with folks who annoy me, give me Your grace not to gloat over people's faults and cover me Lord with Your love to smooth my abrasive edges so that I may more easily work and witness for Jesus.

Forgive us our trespasses
as we forgive those who trespass against us . . .
Matthew 6:12

10th February

'When you pray, go into your room, close the door,
and pray to your Father who is unseen.'

Matthew 6:6

Prayer is so personal: soft-breathed hopes, urgent, silent pleas – and although I know I can pray anywhere, anytime, there is something more definite about going away from the distractions of toys, neighbours passing, washing machine noise; somewhere quiet and alone. I need to be alone otherwise half my prayers are lost . . . Jesus knew how an intrusive world can ruin prayer, He went away to be unhurried, unflustered and to concentrate. Lord, give me a real sense of the power of prayer and the wonderful way it unites christians, and may I realise that my quiet prayer-time gives my life a basis for every day.

Prayer is the burden of a sigh
The falling of a tear;
The upward glancing of an eye
When none but God is near.

James Montgomery

11th February

Sing to the Lord all the earth: proclaim his salvation day after day . . . for great is the Lord, and
most worthy of praise.

1 Chronicles 16:23

Intermingled with all my mundane chores of shopping, ironing, washing-up, my heart is going to sing to the Lord. Thank you Lord for all the comforts and pleasures of my home, for warmth on these cold days, for signs that spring will soon be here, thank you for the strengthening warmth of the February sunshine. When I think of these things it won't be difficult to sing with heart and soul and voice.

I will sing the wondrous story
of the Christ who died for me:
Sing it with the saints in glory
Gathered by the crystal sea.

Francis Ridley Havergal

12th February

Immediately mist and darkness came over him and
he groped about . . .

Acts 13:11

Mist and darkness emotionally and spiritually spells depression. We get covered in the mists of misery, going about in a fog getting nowhere . . . it turns into a real Dumps Day. Nothing and nobody is right and direction has gone from our lives. Yet mist and darkness are only relative . . . way up beyond the sun is still shining – darkness here is dawn in Vancouver or Singapore. Lord, it's time to realise that there is more to the world than me . . .

Father, the moment I lift my eyes towards you, I move from the darkness of self into the light of Your love. The brightness of Your goodness and love melts away anxieties like morning sun on the mists of night.

Frank Topping

13th February

Sarah laughed:

Genesis 18:12

Being in the company of laughter does us good. There is so much misery in the world, such depressing stories in the newspapers, it's a relief to have a good laugh. Sarah's laughter was in disbelief – and today we see many who laugh in disbelief at the christian faith. Lord, we believe that christians will have the last laugh over sceptics and persecutors . . . I pray for the gift of humour to gild life's darker clouds, give me joy that where I live may be a warm haven of fun and pleasantness.

> *Let peace go deep between us all*
> *And joy be shared by everyone:*
> *Laugh and make merry with your friends*
> *And praise the Love that never ends.*

Brian A. Wren

14th February

Why, you don't know what will happen
tomorrow . . .

James 4:14

Joyce was a devoted wife and mother looking forward to the birth of her first grandchild when the doctors diagnosed liver cancer. The disease was too far advanced for any treatment to save her life but they wanted to try some treatment on her; this involved a 70 mile round trip to hospital by ambulance all to no avail. But such was Joyce's faith in her Saviour that she was willing to endure the hospital journeys in the belief that one day it would help sufferers in the future. She knew death would soon release her from the distress of her withered body and she was not afraid. Lord, none of us knows what tomorrow holds . . . strengthen me that come what may, I will not be afraid because I know you will take care of the future.

> *I know not what the future hath*
> *Of marvel or surprise;*
> *Assured alone that life and death*
> *His mercy underlies.*
>
> John Greenleaf Whittier

15th February

Jesus said: 'Go home to your family and tell them how much the Lord has done for you'.

Mark 5:19

On the whole we don't share with our families: oh, yes there are always good reasons why not . . . being too busy scurrying around with domestic commitments, fear of embarrassing them, a state of uneasy truce where a family is reduced to individual bodies who just pass on the stairs. In his work as an assistant chaplain to a prison, Karl Spitta came face to face with the result of broken families, relationships which had gone dead, poisoned by selfishness. He was convinced that the christian message of love and understanding was best learnt within a happy and loving home environment. Lord, forgive me for being hesitant to share my blessings with the family, help me to create a happy and natural atmosphere where all, in your name, are welcome.

> *Happy the home, O loving friend of children,*
> *Where they are given to You with hands of prayer;*
> *Where at Your feet they early learn to listen*
> *To Your own words and thank you for your care.*
>
> Karl Spitta

16th February

O house of Israel, trust in the Lord!

Psalm 113:9

Father, I suppose the truth is that if I have to be reassured by the Bible, challenged by a sermon or reminded to 'trust' by a friend, then it means that, on my own, I lose heart . . . the confidence slips. One big row over breakfast shakes my day and leaves me with a thick, hopeless, choked feeling. Trust in the Lord? . . . well, I try . . . but it's not that easy. I want to trust you Lord – with the unquestioning trust of a small child setting off on a journey with its father; give me Your peace to guide me through joys and tears of today.

> *Not a burden we bear,*
> *Not a sorrow we share,*
> *But our toil He doth richly repay;*
> *Not a grief nor a loss*
> *Not a frown nor a cross*
> *But is blest if we trust and obey.*

John Henry Sammis

17th February

'I have come into the world as a light, so that no-one who believes in me should stay in darkness'.

John 12:46

Visiting a friend's one evening I nearly broke my neck – the street light was out and the steps down from the road to the house became a treacherous black hole. Darkness is disorienting and frightening – although I'd been down those steps many times in daylight, suddenly, in the darkness, I had no idea just where to put my foot. Life for us can be like that when we lose hold of the hand of God. O Lord, who came into this world to bring us the warmth and light of Your presence, draw me into Your light that not only will I know the way, but be able to give a hand to someone else who is still groping in the dark.

Walk in the light: and this shall be
a path, though thorny, bright,
For God by grace shall dwell in thee,
And God himself is Light.

Bernard Barton

18th February

Young and old lie together in the dust of the street.
Lamentations 2:21

It was at Paddington Station I first saw an old woman rummaging in a dustbin. I don't remember her face, only her scruffy stooped outline but what she was doing made a vivid impression on me. We vaguely think of the 'down and out' as old people who have run out of friends and family and have no one to care for them, but today's stark statistics tell us that in our major cities the homeless are both old, and the young. Together they rot in the shadows, under bridges, over gratings, locked in the downward spiral of despair. Lord, once they were all children with dreams and a future, grant that I may hold them up to you in prayer as Your children; thank you for those who will man the hostels and soup kitchens, all who try to make their existence more tolerable . . . bless young and old, lonely and hopeless on our streets this day.

How can you say you're lonely,
And for you that the sun don't shine:
Let me take you by the hand and lead you through the streets of
London,
I'll show you something to make you change your mind.

Tom Paxton

19th February

Mordecai recorded these events, and he sent letters
to all the Jews throughout the provinces . . . near
and far
Esther 9:20

I can think of many people who live long fascinating lives and when they die we realise how little of their life has been recorded – nearly all their memories of history gone for ever. How precious are the odd letters. Indeed, how little we have about Jesus – how precious the early writings of his disciples recording the facts of His life, His death and the resurrection appearances . . . these letters to the early church, keeping them in touch near and far. People long for letters today, to be kept in touch, to be given something fresh to think about – Lord, I love getting letters but I'm so lazy about writing them; if I've been putting off a letter perhaps today is the right time to get down to it, to keep in touch . . .

See what large letters I use as I write to you with my own hand! . . .
The grace of our Lord Jesus Christ be with your spirit, brothers.
Amen.
Paul in his letter to the Galations
6:11 & 18

20th February

Moses summoned Joshua and said to him . . . 'The
Lord himself goes before you and will be with you;
he will never leave you nor forsake you . . .
Deuteronomy 31:7/8

When prominent people in society retire a frenzied cry breaks out as 'how shall we manage . . .' It is totally unreasonable to depend on one person to such an extent but in all walks of life it happens and one of the most valuable lessons to learn is that nobody is indispensible! Joshua had depended on Moses all the years in the wilderness – nobody could imagine how to cope without having Moses around to moan at. Wise old Moses spoke words for Joshua which I can take with me for today – people come and go, governments rise and fall, but God is always with us. Dear Lord, help me not to place all my faith and aspirations in a person, but show me how to put all my trust in Jesus.

Never leave me nor forsake me
Ever be my friend,
For I need Thee from life's dawning
To its end.

Walter J. Mathams

21st February

For he will command his angels concerning you to
guard you in all your ways . . .

Psalm 91:11

Many people in our community act as angels . . . bearers of goodness and help in the face of harsh, unkind, often unfair reality.
Lord, thank you for the angels working in the hospitals, for the
home-helps, ambulance drivers, fire-men, the staff of hospices
and residential homes for children and the elderly. I am overwhelmed by the unstinting kindness, patience and care of these
men and women for the lives in their charge. Help me Lord to
forget the cardboard and tinsel-type angel of distant nativities –
make me aware of the positive power of gentleness, of angels'
work here on earth.

I believe in angels because the Bible says there are angels: and I
believe the Bible to be the true Word of God. I also believe in
angels because I have sensed their presence in my life on special
occasions.

Billy Graham

22nd February

I pray that you may be active in sharing your
faith . . .

Philemon 6

To be in love is to want to shout the name of our loved one
everywhere, and all the time – we think of little else. The golfing

enthusiast will endure any loathesome weather to play a round or watch a professional; the C.B. radio buff, the breaker with personal handle, can't leave the radio alone . . . yes, we all know how time flies when we are sharing a little world of personal pleasure. Lord, I need to pray for enthusiasm for the Gospel, may it become so richly alive in my life that I can share my faith without feeling awkward or strange; guide my life so that my enthusiasm may be catching and bring someone else to share their faith too.

I recognise, as we all have to do, that Christianity must mean everything to us before it can mean anything to others.

Lord Soper

23rd February

Then the man who had received one talent came:
'Master', he said 'I was afraid and went and hid
your talent in the ground'.

Matthew 25:24

How often do we see talent go to waste because of lack of perseverance, a couldn't-care-less attitude, downright idleness? To make the best use of the talents God has given to us will take time, energy, patience and dedication and in the story in Matthew's gospel, Jesus points out that it is wrong to waste our gifts. It just won't do to think we can turn to Jesus and say, 'Oh, well, I didn't think it mattered'. Each one of us has a gift for something – for listening, for soothing, for teaching or building up; we have no right to say to God we have nothing to offer, we have. Lord, all my abilities I offer to You that You can use me for Your name to be glorified.

My talents, gifts and graces, Lord,
Into Thy blessed hand receive.

Charles Wesley

24th February

Come near to God and He will come near to you.

James 4:8

There is no point in being stand-offish with God: no faith can grow if God is only wheeled on stage for an hour a week. As with any relationship there has to be a good two-way understanding which deepens and grows out of continual contact. If we love someone, we want to be with them but we never get to know what a stranger likes. Lord, I am sorry that at times you get pushed to the back of a hectic day; help me to find more time to talk to you while I'm waiting for a bus, waiting for the children to come home or doing the ironing and don't let me forget that I need to listen too. I want that two-way exchange . . . I want to be close to Jesus.

Draw me nearer, nearer, nearer blessed Lord,
To Thy precious, bleeding side.

Frances Jane Van Alstyne

25th February

Jesus and his disciples went on to the villages around Caesarea Philippi. . . . On the way He asked them: 'Who do you say that I am?'

Mark 8:29

Over the years Jesus has been dubbed everything from spaceman to revolutionary. Even those who deny His divinity accept that He was a charismatic figure, an outstanding teacher and seeker after a truly harmonious world. Christians down the centuries have come to know Jesus as a living presence within their lives which has transformed them; there has been a revolution in their lives, a new concern for all mankind. I believe in our society of sceptics, of great arguments and doubt, of sincere searching for a better way of life, Jesus stops me in my tracks to ask those same words . . . 'Who do you say that I am?' Lord, if I can say like Peter, You are the Christ! then there has been a rebirth of my soul.

Jesus puts us to the tasks which He has to carry out in our age. He commands. And to those who obey, be they wise or simple, He will reveal Himself through all that they are privileged to experience in His fellowship of peace and activity, of struggle and suffering, till they come to know, as an inexpressible secret, who He is . . .

Albert Schweitzer

26th February

I sought the Lord and he answered me: he delivers
me from all my fears.

Psalm 34:4

I was sent a poem once which said, in a nutshell, there's so much to do in life there simply isn't time to pray. The anonymous poet then goes on to wonder why God lets things become so hard – doesn't he care? isn't he there? The answer at the end of the poem is that we have become so busy that we have ignored God who has been there all the time. Loving Heavenly Father, forgive me for the times when I've not sought You, I've not bothered to ask for guidance but crashed on in my own strength only to get into a mess. I'm seeking you now, Lord . . . I need you so much.

. . . if you seek the Lord your God, you will find Him if you look for Him with all your heart and with all your soul. For the Lord your God is a merciful God, He will not abandon or destroy you . . .

Deuteronomy 4: 29 & 31

27th February

Worthy is the Lamb who was slain

Revelations 5:12

Ray Palmer's first job was in a grain merchant's store – not the most likely place to get inspiration for a poem, but in his early twenties Ray wrote a poem which he was to carry in his wallet for many years. He studied, and became an ordained minister: then one day two men came along to his church who were compiling a new hymn-book. They asked the minister if he had any suggestions to offer; from his wallet Ray produced the poem which was to become a much-loved hymn on both sides of the Atlantic. Lord, I must learn that if I do something in Your name, I must not demand instant results . . . in Your good time words written, spoken or sung with Love, will bear fruit.

> *My faith looks up to Thee*
> *Thou Lamb of Calvary, Saviour Divine:*
> *Now hear me while I pray; take all my guilt away;*
> *O let me from this day be wholly Thine.*

Ray Palmer

28th February

Jesus went into Galilee proclaiming the Good News of God. 'The time has come,' he said, 'The Kingdom of God is near . . . '

Mark 1:14

Jesus preached to change attitudes. Religious leaders had become entrenched in tradition, separate from sinners . . . Jesus was up against bigotry, double-standards, political intrigue, racial hatred, ignorance and poverty alongside great learning, privilege and affluence. Situations known to every generation in every part of the world – He comes still, with good news, offering a better life . . . O Lord God, what a fantastic world this could be with every tongue confessing the name of Jesus: today my prayer is 'Thy Kingdom come'.

> *Thy kingdom come O God*
> *Thy rule O Christ begin:*
> *Break with Thine iron rod,*
> *The tyrannies of sin.*

Lewis Hensley

29th February

Now we see but a poor reflection; then we shall see
face to face. Now I know in part, then I shall know
fully, even as I am fully known.

1 Corinthians 13:12

The newspaper report said that a baby had been abandoned on a doorstep and the estimate was that it was only an hour old. Lord, how do people get themselves into such a tangle? It's so sad when we see lives in a mess . . . we are all such frail human beings, so prone to the ensnaring grasp of seemingly insolvable problems. As I pray for those I know who can't see clearly which way to turn, I'm reminded of the embroidered book-mark in my Bible: to see it on one side is to see coloured threads in a higgeldy-piggeldy fashion. There is no order, nothing which makes sense on the underside, but when I turn it over, there the coloured threads are perfectly embroidered into 'God is Love'. Lord, give me the faith to carry on knowing that although I can't see a solution, or a pattern emerging, You are the unseen presence which shapes and supports me until one day, my vision will understand, my heart will adore and my soul sing.

> *And then when Jesus face to face I see*
> *When at his lofty throne I bow the knee,*
> *Then of his love in all its breadth and length*
> *Its height and depth and everlasting strength*
> *My soul shall sing.*

Mary Shekleton

1st March

For we do not preach ourselves, but Jesus Christ as
Lord.

Corinthians 2:4; 5

We are all such a mixture of backgrounds, age, a hotch-potch of opinions and prejudices and we get so puzzled and put-out when people don't agree with us. Today Lord, I recall another line from the 14th. century nun's prayer 'teach me the glorious lesson that I may be mistaken' . . . Forgive me that I do slip into the habit of putting forward my own ideas and principles when I ought to know better and offer only Jesus as Lord. Jesus, the name above all names, Jesus the Lord over all our silly man-made denominations, Jesus – my Lord and my God.

Jesus is Lord, o'er sin the mighty conqueror,
From death He rose, and all His foes shall own His name;
Jesus is Lord, God sends His Holy Spirit
To show by works of power that Jesus is Lord.
Jesus is Lord, Jesus is Lord
praise Him with alleluias for Jesus is Lord.

David Mansell

2nd March

Jesus answered: 'I am the way and the truth and the life. No-one comes to the Father except through me'.

John 14:6

A little boy with only two years education behind him was dragged off to sea. He learnt to receive and later inflict brutality, he swore in every breath and for six years he was in charge of a slave ship. A harder nut to crack would have been difficult to find – but John Newton met Jesus. He studied for several years before being ordained into the church of England at the age of 39 and his church was a little country parish in Buckinghamshire. At this church John Newton began weekly prayer meetings for which he wrote many hymns; he speaks through his poetry of the personal Jesus who rescued him from such a debauched life; he speaks of the Jesus who will meet our individual needs if we but look to Him. Lord Jesus – soothe my sorrow, heal my wounds, and drive away my fear.

Jesus my Shepherd, Brother, Friend,
My Prophet, Priest and King;
My Lord, my Life, my Way, my End
Accept the praise I bring.

John Newton

3rd March

You turned my wailing into dancing; you removed
my sackcloth and clothed me with joy that my
heart may sing to you . . .'

Psalm 30:11/12

I watched a small girl of about eight years old jump out of the family car to join her friends on the way into a Disco. In a bounce of uninhibited girlish joy she danced and skipped her way to the waiting group. How beautiful to be young and carefree – how sad so many of us have forgotten how to dance! Lord, I remember You said that we must accept the kingdom of heaven like children – so today I pray for that inner happiness which may lead to a spontaneous leap for the sheer joy of being alive.

My God, I am Thine,
What a comfort divine
What a blessing to know that my Jesus is mine.
In the heavenly Lamb
Thrice happy I am,
And my heart it doth dance at the sound of His name.

Charles Wesley

4th March

The men were amazed and asked: 'What kind of
man is this? Even the winds and waves obey Him?'

Matthew 8:27

In the gospel accounts of the many miracles Jesus performed it is pretty obvious that the disciples never really came to terms with the unearthly power Jesus demonstrated. In the calming of the sea, the sheer amazement of the men comes over as forcibly as the miracle itself. Lord, I'm guilty too – on one hand I believe Your almighty power but on the other hand I don't expect to see it. Your ways are a mystery but I know that you will calm the storms inside my head, I know that as the wind, Your power is unseen, but I see it's evidence . . . be with me in doubt and trembling . . . move in my triumphs and joys.

God moves in a mysterious way
His wonders to perform,
He plants His footsteps in the sea
And rides upon the storm.

William Cowper

5th March

Our offences and sins weigh us down. As surely as I
live, declares the Sovereign Lord, I take no pleasure
in the death of the wicked, but rather that they turn
from their ways and live. Turn from your evil way!
Ezekiel 33:10

Newspapers have become a depressing catalogue of evil and
sometimes the television news is so distressing, I can't watch.
Surely, we do seem weighed down by all the horror about us and
we find ourselves screeching for revenge – calling for these wicked
people to be obliterated from the rest of humane society . . . It's so
hard Lord to be objective: to learn to divorce the sin from the
sinner. And here, in the prophet Ezekiel's revelation, I see that
You don't want the wicked destroyed, but You long for them to
change their hearts. I need to learn that when things seem impossible to me, nothing is beyond Your power, and what's more,
no-one is beyond Your love.

Turn back, oh man, forswear thy foolish ways . . .

Clifford Bax

6th March

The Lord is near: do not be anxious about anything.
Philippians 4:5

The essence of this verse is 'Don't worry'. It's laughable that the
Word of God holds so many promises of comfort for us yet the

world's growth industry is Worry! Agony Aunts in every magazine, putrid little horoscopes in the newspapers, radio phone-ins . . . all swamped with our insurmountable problems. We can't think straight sometimes for the worry that is gnawing at our very souls. O Lord, I do so much want to feel you near; I remember the hymn which says 'be with me when no other friend the secret of my heart can share –' I pray for your nearness now. I am physically exhausted with worrying – fill me with your strength that I can break through the cloud of my burden – help me to smile as I lay my anxieties down.

> *Don't worry what you have to say*
> *Don't worry, because on that day*
> *God's spirit will speak in your heart . . .*

Alan T. Dale

7th March

Jesus said to them: ' . . . the poor you will always
have with you . . .'

Matthew 26:11

The very fact that every society has a sad proportion of poor people pushes them to the edge of our day to day consciousness. Lord, forgive me that I don't care enough – that worship consists of remembering the poor by the odd recollection, a passing pious hope; show me that words and thoughts are not enough and etch the words of James into my heart: 'suppose a brother or sister is without clothes and daily food. If one of you says, Go, I wish you well – but does nothing about his physical need, what good is that? Faith, if not accompanied by action is dead'. Lord, what good have I done? Is my faith comatose? sickly? or is it a vital, living force in my day?

If we can put ourselves in the shoes of the poor and disadvantaged, we may see how matters appear to their consciousness – matters which affect the whole of our society. They are to do with God taking flesh in the person of Jesus, living out His life in a special relation to the poor.

David Sheppard

8th March

'Even now,' declares the Lord, 'Return to me with
all your heart, with fasting, weeping and mourn-
ing.'

Joel 2:12

It is never too late to return to God – not if we are truly sorry; our
Heavenly Father is however, not interested in vague apologies,
limp-wristed excuses with little effort or resolve behind them; He
wants us to return to Him with real tears. The amazing thing is
that He does want us . . . Lord, I weep for my stupidity, even of
today, never mind yesterday . . . I come to leave my past at the
foot of the Cross.

> *O come and mourn with me awhile,*
> *O come ye to the Saviour's side:*
> *O come, together let us mourn*
> *Jesus, our Lord, is crucified.*
>
> Frederick William Faber

9th March

'You grumbled in your tents . . . "our brothers
have made us lose heart" . . . '

Deuteronomy 1:27

What a mob! Poor old Moses leading the Israelites to the
Promised Land and all the thanks he got was wailing and back-
biting. Everything was wrong – even the food wasn't as good as it
had been in Egypt! Can't you just hear their mutterings . . . 'it's
not as good as it used to be . . . ' Yes, Lord, what a lot we have to
learn. We grumble away like dripping taps because things are
different, not as we remember them and want them to always stay
– and how we so easily bend to the disparaging influence of
others. Now I can see it, help me to take a grip on myself so that
today, with Your help, I will not grumble.

*Therefore, since through God's mercy we have this ministry, we
do not lose heart!*

2 Corinthians 4:1

10th March

The Lord said to Abraham 'Leave your country,
and your people and your father's household and
go to the land I will show you'.

Genesis 12:1

Leaving 'home' is traumatic. A step into the unknown – different
faces, strange buildings, fresh routines, we don't want to leave all
the family and things we know behind. But then, literally thousands of people face the prospect of leaving home each week –
perhaps to look for a job, to begin a new job, to get married, to
escape a relationship, to go to college or university or to give up
home for sheltered accommodation. Each move is a step along
life's chequer board. Lord, I need Abraham's faith, to feel deep
down, underneath all the heart flutterings of anticipation or
doubt, that wherever I go You are with me and after all, strangers
are only friends I have not yet met.

> *What He says we will do*
> *Where He sends we will go,*
> *Never fear, only trust and obey.*

John Henry Sammis

11th March

Because of the increase of wickedness, the love of
most will grow cold . . .

Matthew 24:12

I know I can't hold on to mountain-top experiences and all of us
get our 'highs' and 'lows' but I do feel so guilty when my love for
husband and family droops. My enthusiasm flags under the
pressure of a hundred urgent demands on my time, patience,
emotions and ordered routine. Wickedness appears to be increasing daily, held up in the newspapers, T.V., films, videos, dreadful
statistics of violence and language loaded with hate. Is it any
wonder love grows cold? Jesus knows my human nature, knows
my selfishness and heart-breaking fickleness . . . and still he loves
me. Lord, I must hang on to Love.

When shall all hatred cease?
When comes the promised time when war shall be no more?
Men scorn Thy sacred name: by many deeds of shame
We learn that love grows cold.

Lewis Hensley

12th March

Jesus said: 'I am the good shepherd: I know my
sheep and my sheep know me'.

John 10:14

The television series called One Man and His Dog has given new
insight into the often quoted words of Jesus, it has brought the
picture of sheep and shepherd right into our living rooms. And
how like sheep we are – some docile, willing to be driven along in
a close-knit group while every so often you pick out a defiant ewe
whose influence ends up scattering the lot of them. So Jesus spoke
about His flock – we all need to be guided, cared for – we can
know Jesus and he knows each one of us. Lord and master,
kindest shepherd, gather me into your fold . . . I am listening for
Your still, calm voice within my heart.

It takes a bit of accepting when Jesus says that sheep know the
shepherd's voice and the shepherd knows his sheep individually –
can any man and animal have a relationship as close as that? Well,
now I know they can – I've seen it.

John Jackson (on Sheep Dog Trials)

13th March

An angel of the Lord said to Philip: 'Go south to the
road . . . the desert road . . . that goes down from
Jerusalem to Gaza.'

Acts 8:26

We've all experienced times when we've intended to do one thing,
go in a certain direction, then all of a sudden there comes that

inner voice telling us to do something quite different. I believe it is the guidance of the Holy Spirit directing our lives. Lord, today I pray that I may be receptive to the guidance You direct, may faith brighten my way and may I be used, like Philip, to speak to someone of Jesus.

So shall my walk be close with God
Calm and serene my frame;
So purer light shall mark the road
That leads me to the Lamb.

William Cowper

14th March

Search me, O God, and know my heart; test me and know my anxious thoughts; see if there be any offensive way in me and lead me in the way everlasting.

Psalm 139:23

Lord, I am ashamed of my secret thoughts – the darker side of my nature which seems to lurk waiting to take over when I'm trying my best to be kind and thoughtful. Lord, you see into my heart and mind as no-one else, you see me warts and all . . . help me, fill me with new life and thoughts until there is no room for anything else but your goodness.

Search me O God and know my heart today . . .
I praise Thee Lord, for cleansing me from sin,
Fulfil Thy word and make me pure within;
Fill me with fire, where once I burned with shame,
Grant my desire to magnify Thy name.

J. Edwin Orr

15th March

You cannot fast as you do today and expect your
voice to be heard on high . . .

Isaiah 58:4

Lord, what a farce we tend to make of Lent. To give up sweets – go without sugar – give up smoking . . . how vain and small-minded can we be! Like children who turn off the bedroom light and then carry on reading by torch-light under the bedclothes, so we manage to cling on to all that we love to indulge in, under the cover of Lenten piety. As I read the fifty-eighth chapter of Isaiah, I realise that the sacrifice my God requires is the elimination of oppression, a sharing of food resources, striving for justice and recognition of the worth of each individual. This is the true search, this is the path to the Kingdom of Heaven. Lord, forgive me that my vision is woefully stilted – as I study Your Word, may this time of Lent truly prepare my soul and my life.

'Let us approach our Lenten acts of self-denial with the right sort of attitude, an attitude which will allow the Lord into some of our problem areas to rescue us and save us . . . '

Delia Smith

16th March

'Have faith in God,' Jesus answered

Mark 11:12

Rose Kennedy, the matriarch of the Kennedy clan, endured through her long life more than her fair share of public and private tragedy within her rich and glamorous family. Yet she stated that she placed her faith as her most precious gift. We can look at the Kennedy story as a modern parable to see that it doesn't matter how much money, influence, power or star-quality you possess, you never know when you may be touched by scandal, drugs, illness or anything else which reduces wordly gifts to nothing. We are all vulnerable . . . we all need that special something we call faith. Lord, I pray that the wisdom of Rose Kennedy will rub off on my day, help me to nurture, treasure and strengthen my faith.

> *My faith it is an oaken staff*
> *O let me on it lean . . .*
>
> Thomas T. Lynch

17th March

Cast all your anxiety on Him because He cares for
you.

1 Peter 5:7

To stand and watch a row of shoppers standing at the check-out, or groups of people standing or sitting around in airport lounges, is to feel the world is full of anxious faces. I suppose there is so much to be anxious about . . . mortgage, unemployment, tension in marriage, tension at work, loneliness . . . I trudge through the day under a shroud of problems. Heavenly Father how slow I am – the New Testament writers couldn't have put things more plainly as they teach me to bring all my anxieties to Jesus; it won't make them disappear, but I'll be able to get them into proportion and I'll be able to cope. Lord, help me to believe in my heart what my eyes read.

> *All your anxiety, all your care, bring to the mercy seat –*
> *Leave it there;*
> *Never a burden He cannot bear – never a friend like Jesus!*
>
> E. H. Joy

18th March

Now that I, your Lord and Teacher have washed
your feet, you also should wash one another's feet.

John 13:14

There are times when I know I'm happy to avoid the menial job – it's easy to leave it to someone else. Show me, Lord, the greatness, the wideness of the love that is willing to serve; oh for the humility to live in this way. I pray that today will see me taking my part in the office, the job-centre, shop, market place and home with common courtesy, kindliness and open friendliness and if Jesus, my Lord and Saviour, could serve His followers, then I have to learn there is nothing I should refuse to do for others.

> *Kneel at the feet of our friends*
> *Silently washing their feet:*
> *This is the way we should live with You*
> *Jesus, Jesus, fill us with your love —*
> *Show us how to serve the neighbours we have from You.*

T. S. Colvin
based on a song from N. Ghana

19th March

Jesus turned and saw her, 'Take heart, daughter'
He said, 'Your faith has healed you.'

Matthew 9:22

If only we could take the billions of bottles of medicines, pills, ointments, potions, etc, etc, and put them on a bonfire because everyone had been healed of their pain and suffering. The young mother crippled with rheumatoid arthritis, the father with multiple sclerosis, the widow who cannot sleep without her sleeping pills . . . countless thousands of people so sick in heart, mind and body. Today, Lord, I come to You to say thank you for all the methods of alleviating pain, the advances in medical science, the skill of the surgeons, and for those I know who are sick, I pray for Your healing touch, either in this world or in the life to come where there won't be any crying, nor any pain.

> *Thou O Christ art all I want,*
> *More than all in Thee I find:*
> *Raise the fallen, cheer the faint,*
> *Heal the sick and lead the blind.*

Charles Wesley

20th March

See! The winter is past: the rains are over and gone.
Flowers appear on the earth, the season of singing
has come.

Songs of Songs 2

Yes, the winter is past . . . the first snowdrops, primroses and wood anemones, violets and budding trees all herald the returning miracle of Spring. When I take the trouble to look I can see signs of new life everywhere – all the deadness and coldness is disappearing and the birds are singing above the urban traffic and nesting in the country lanes. Reawakening! Time to clear away the winter debris and plan for spring planting . . . time too to refresh my sight with the wonder of the changing seasons. Lord, words of thanks seem inadequate, praise goes nowhere in expressing how I feel, but You know the difference it makes to have the winter behind me, so I offer my happiness as worship.

The glory of the Spring how sweet,
The new-born life how glad,
What joy the happy earth to greet
In new, bright raiment clad.

Thomas Hornblower Gill

21st March

During those days another large crowd gathered.
Since they had nothing to eat, Jesus called his disciples and said 'I have compassion for these
people.'

Mark 8:1

In our affluent times of 'take-aways' and food shops around every corner, it's beyond us to imagine a crowd going off to listen to a teacher with nothing to eat. I suppose, Lord, I'm preoccupied with eating but I draw one strand of truth from this story: it was the crowd's very dependence upon Jesus that aroused His compassion . . . they had nothing. Lord, I may have heaps to eat and all sorts of material blessings, yet teach me that before Jesus, I have nothing and fill my emptiness with Your love.

Nothing in my hand I bring –
Simply to Thy cross I cling.
Augustus M. Toplady

22nd March

We are under great pressure, far beyond our ability
to endure, so that we despaired even of life – but
this happened that we might not rely on ourselves,
but on God.

2 Corinthians 1:8

I look at some people and I wonder how they cope with the
pressures life brings; sometimes I feel I can't cope with my own.
The Samaritans are experiencing a great increase in people who
are driven to despair, and a large slice of them being teenagers. So,
despair is by no means unique, and not a phenomenon of the
present age . . . when people look to themselves it's always the
same. Paul learnt that he only had Jesus to rely on and that peace
and calm assurance brought him through hostility, prison and
ship-wreck. Those things are not likely to happen to me today, but
Lord, make me a better person by learning to rely on Your
strength.

Faith is a great art and doctrine which no saint has learned and
fully fathomed unless he has found himself in despair.

Martin Luther

23rd March

And rain fell on the earth 40 days and 40 nights.

Genesis 7:12

Sometimes I look out of my window and feel like shouting: 'If it
rains any more Lord, I shall scream!' Look at my pile of washing –

how am I supposed to keep the floor clean – what can I do with the children, the dog, the cat . . . ?' Being wet makes me miserable. Time for some positive thinking . . . Thank you, Lord, that rain means full reservoirs, clean water from the tap, water for industry, for crops and animals. Help me to feel refreshed after rain, to see roofs shining and delicate droplets hanging on cobwebs. Soothing, life-supporting rain . . . and didn't Jesus offer water? Living Water . . .

'*Whoever drinks of the water I shall give will never thirst; the water I shall give will become in him a spring of water welling up to Eternal Life.*'

John 4:14

24th March

Now, who is willing to concentrate himself today
to the Lord?

1 Chronicles 29:5

An easy question to answer when surrounded by a large congregation, addressed by a dynamic speaker able to lead many to the point of decision: far different a question when we're on our own, or with friends who aren't interested in the Gospel. Dear Lord, I am as fickle as the crowd which followed Jesus into Jerusalem; with the right crowd I'll shout my hozannas, but with others I'd rather melt into the background and say nothing. Today, Lord, I ask for courage – courage to make the right decisions and to consecrate myself for Your work, never to be shame-faced in any company.

> *Consecrate me now to Thy service lord,*
> *By the power of grace divine;*
> *Let my soul look up with a steadfast hope*
> *And my will be lost in Thine.*

Frances Jane van Alstyne

25th March

I will sprinkle clean water on you and you will be
clean . . .

Ezekiel 36:25

The tireless apostle Paul declared to his listeners that everyone
had sinned and fallen short of the glory of God . . . the respectable
citizens didn't like it . . . nor do I – but it is the truth that hurts. In
this time of Lent I realise more than ever my need to be cleansed;
when my devotions have become jaded and my prayers dry,
Almighty and Redeeming Lord, have mercy on me, a sinner who
needs Your sprinkling of clean water.

*The water may be symbolic but the cleansing is real: just as we
need to wash our bodies to get rid of the dust and dirt of our daily
life, so spiritually the same thing needs to happen – we can
become very dusty spiritually.*

Delia Smith

26th March

Jesus said: 'Greater love has no man than this, that
one lay down his life for his friends.'

John 15:13

Why is the word 'Love' so trivialised today? We say – I love going
to the theatre, I love sweet and sour pork, I love walking the
dog . . . such diverse emotions claiming the same word. So you
see, Lord, it's hard to come to terms with real love, the love that
demands self-sacrifice – because we are too occupied with ourselves. The singer Mary O'Hara wrote in her biography about the
terminal illness of her young husband and she was able to say that
the more she loved her husband, the more she was able to love
God. Perhaps this is the day for me to forget myself and in loving
care for others, step beyond myself into the everlasting arms of
Love.

Our every feverish mood is cooled
And gone is every load,
When we can lose the love of self
And find the love of God.   Benjamin Waugh

27th March

Children's children are a crown to the aged.
Proverbs 17:8

How true the old proverb can be — grandparents are absolutely thrilled with the arrival of grandchildren — their lives become willingly transformed into renewed activities . . . knitting, erecting swings, walks in the park, paddles at the seaside, days out and nights in to babysit. Then there are the treasured photos capturing the christening, the first tooth, first steps, first day at school, sports day achievements and so on. Grandparents are 'special' because they have time. Time to play, time to answer the endless questions and time to recount stories of 'long ago' . . . it's a special, two-way relationship which enriches both generations. Lord, thank you for these relationships . . . and my prayers are for those where through broken marriages, the closeness between grandparents and grandchildren has gone sour and they are strangers.

May young and old together find
In Christ the Lord of every day:
That fellowships our homes may bind
In joy and sorrow, work and play.
Parents and children, may we live
In glad obedience, Lord, to Thee.   Hugh Martin

28th March

Elijah came to a broom tree, sat down under it and
prayed that he might die. 'I've had enough, Lord'
he said.

1 Kings 19:4

It's easy to be patronising towards Elijah – he'd witnessed God's power and protection yet there he was, miserably hiding away, all depressed and hopeless. Everything was alright in the end, but at that particular point, he didn't have the confidence to go on . . . but now then, just a moment – how often have I said 'I've had enough'?? I've had my miseries too . . . . Time to pull up my spiritual socks, I won't sit down under things like poor old Elijah, because I have the promises of Jesus that I shall never be alone. O Lord, forgive my shallow reserves, pick me up from under my broom tree and show me that I am part of Your fascinating and challenging world . . . Life is worth Living!

> *How blest is life if lived for Thee*
> *To feel that though I journey on*
> *By stony paths and rugged ways,*
> *Thy blessed feet have gone before,*
> *And strength is given for weary days.*

Anonymous

29th March

Near the cross of Jesus stood his mother.

John 19:25

Mary had experienced more than anyone else with Jesus. There had been the fear mingled with sublime joy at the birth of her first born . . . her son; then he had frustrated and puzzled her by his attitude to her and Joseph when they found him in the Temple on the verge of his teens . . . (and what mother hasn't felt those emotions when confronted by the emergence of her child's independence!). She had laughed, cried and depended upon Jesus – she had been so proud of him, so afraid for him, then the final agony of watching her wonderful son dying. A mother – bearing all things. Lord, every woman can identify with the heights and depths of Mary's experiences . . . bless every mother today with patience, limitless understanding and a sense of fun.

When Jesus saw his mother there, and the disciple whom he loved standing by, he said to his mother: 'Dear Woman, here is your son'. And to the disciple, 'Here is your mother'. From that time on, this disciple took her into his home.

John 19:26/27

30th March

Mary of Magdala went to the disciples with the news: 'I have seen the Lord!'

John 20:18

There are times when we are all guilty of plodding through the day with eyes 'down': we are preoccupied to the point of clouding out the ability to look up and 'see' ... Lord I want to look up and away from the petty bickerings in families, between neighbours, from political nastiness and verbal back-stabbing, help me to raise my sights to see what really matters today. Give me an awareness of all the good that is going on, in Day Centres and Rehabilitation homes, ordinary people caring for ordinary people, and thereby sharing the good news of Christ's love in the hearts, the Risen Lord appearing through the serving life.

> *Came Mary to that Garden*
> *And sobbed with heart forlorn ...*
> *She heard her own name spoken*
> *And then she lost her care —*
> *The Risen Lord stood there.*

Alda M. Milner-Barry

31st March

Your God reigns!

Isaiah 52:7b

What a tiny speck my life is! Who knows me ten minutes down the road? and what's more, who cares? No Prince or President would bother to look in on me for coffee; sometimes it seems pointless even to hold opinions as they make no impact whatsoever on anyone and the world revolves in total disregard to whether I'm happy or sad. Thank you Lord that whatever happens, whether governments come and go, whether my day is smooth or completely turned upside down, whether churches and theologians are breathing fire at one another, through everything You are God You are changeless, You will reign for ever and ever, Amen.

When we deliberate, He reigns; when we decide wisely, He reigns; when we decide foolishly, He reigns: when we serve Him in humble loyalty, He reigns;
When we rebel and seek to withhold our service, He reigns;
He reigns – the Alpha and Omega . . . the Almighty.

William Temple

1st April

'When you fast, do not look sombre as the hypocrites do . . . when you fast put oil on your head and wash your face, so that it will not be obvious to men that you are fasting.'

Matthew 6:16

Such a temptation to make sure everyone knows when we are making a minor sacrifice . . . Lord, if I use this age-old method of discipline, help me to remember it is not for the good of my health but I fast to heighten my awareness of all that is wrong within my life: the grudges I don't forget, the ill-feeling, deep-rooted bitterness, wraps of self-righteousness. Jesus, my Saviour, went alone to fast, to prepare Himself for the sacrifice of living and finally dying for ungrateful humanity. Lord, prepare me, chasten me and keep me cheerful today.

How can Your pardon reach and bless
  The unforgiving heart
That broods on wrongs, and will not let old bitterness depart?

Rosamond Herklots

2nd April

Peter replied: 'Even if all fall away on account of you, I never will . . . even if I have to die with you, I will never disown you'.

Matthew 26:33

Anyone who has owned a dog knows that unfaltering loyalty, the heart-warming assurance that we shall always receive the most joyful of welcomes. Few people have that kind of reliability . . . our best intentions drain into oblivion at the slightest obstacle. Peter was so definite he would follow Jesus, no matter what . . . not even death could stop him . . . not until he stood alone, frightened and taunted by a girl. O Lord, what would I have done? Forgive me for being a good starter but a poor finisher – I pray for loyalty, courage and perseverance in all my work and if I make a bold public statement, give me strength to see it through to the end.

Here we learn to serve and give,
and, rejoicing, self-deny;
Here we gather love to live
Here we gather faith to die.

Elizabeth Rundle Charles

3rd April

For the Day of the Lord is near, in the valley of decision.

Joel 3:14

When a General Election looms, the media leaps with expectation at the see-sawing opinion polls. However, the aspect of these polls that catches my eye is the section devoted to the 'Don't Knows'. Do they ever make up their minds? or do they ignore the polling booths . . . ? Lord, it is easier and less hassle to sit on the fence, to fudge my true ideals so as not to upset someone, but I pray that I don't become a spiritual Don't Know – give me the courage, and strength of faith to make the right decisions, to stay by Jesus the Way, the Truth and the Life.

> *Once to every man and nation*
> *Comes the moment to decide*
> *In the strife of truth with falsehood,*
> *For the good or evil side.*

James Russell Lowell

4th April

Jesus said to them: 'Have you never read the Scriptures?'

Matthew 21:42

I was rushing to complete a DIY decorating job and chose a new brand of paint. I knew about paint so I didn't read the instructions – I sanded down, undercoated and finally used the new gloss paint. With the job finished I looked at the side of the empty tin and read: 'this paint needs no undercoat'. Several times Jesus made remarks to the Pharisees about reading the scriptures which must have made them wild – they above all people were the ones who were soaked in every syllable of the Scriptures – no travelling preacher could tell them anything! Lord, however many times I've looked at a portion of the Bible, I ask for fresh eyes to read what Your Word has to say to me.

> *We read Thy power to bless and save*
> *E'en in the darkness of the grave:*
> *Still more in resurrection light*
> *We read the fullness of Thy might.*

Horatius Bonar

5th April

... and when the Sabbath came, Jesus went into
the Synagogue

Mark 1:21

From a small boy Jesus had been in the Synagogue every Sabbath, listening to the Rabbis reading the Holy Scriptures, learning of the sufferings of the Jewish nation, learning of the way in which God had led them at every turn. Lord, as I go to worship, I shall hear the same Old Testament stories as Jesus heard, but also I shall hear of how Jesus, through his resurrected life will be with me at every turn in the power and comfort of His Holy Spirit. What ever the day brings I will worship with gladness, I will rejoice and sing ...

> *Jesus stand among us in Thy risen power*
> *Let this time of worship be a hallowed hour.*
> *Breath the Holy Spirit into every heart,*
> *Bid the fears and sorrows from each soul depart.*
>
> William Pennefeather

6th April

His disciples had gone into the town to buy food.

John 4:8

Well – how interesting to come across a domestic insight into the chores which affected Jesus and his disciples – even these men, destined to turn the world upside down, had to go shopping! Dear Lord and Creator of all, thank you for the strength to do my own shopping, thank you for all the different variety of stores and foods undreamt of a few decades ago. My fridge, freezer and cupboards hold the harvest of scores of countries all around the world – I am richly blessed – Lord, give me grace to remember how fortunate I am the next time I grouse about yet another shopping trip.

> *We thank you O God for Your goodness,*
> *For the joy and abundance of crops;*
> *For food that is stored in our larders,*
> *For all we can buy in the shops.*
>
> Fred Kaan

7th April

The Lord will watch over your coming and going:

Psalm 121:8

Travelling on the bus I see literally hundreds of comings and goings – postmen, milkmen, school children, shop assistants and business men, all dashing along like so many anonymous ants. Everyone with a different thought: the paperboy needing more revision time for his exams, the lonely pensioner on the way to the Post Office, the district nurse on her way home from a patient . . . on the bus from that detached distance I stare at faces I will never see again, but the Lord watches over each and every one of us, closer than breathing. Lord, it's comforting to know You are there . . .

As I travel through the bad and good,
Keep me travelling the way I should;
And it's from the old I travel to the new –
Keep me travelling along with you.   Sydney Carter

8th April

Jesus said 'Look at the birds of the air . . . see how
the lilies of the field grow . . .'

Matthew 6:26/28

A blackbird has been singing outside my back door for days – from first glint of dawn to evening – a rich, happy song of spring! It's done me good to hear him, just an ordinary blackbird, whose only teacher to sing, build nests and bring up the young is the divine miracle of instinct. Then, as I look from primrose to cherry blossom, I see each petal is a miniature wonder, even the grass pushing up through the cracks in the pavement reminds me of the strength of Life. Yes, Lord, I believe you created these flowers and creatures which brighten my day, and surely, if I stop to notice how they bloom and grow, sing and fly all by themselves, then I shall know beyond a shadow of doubt, that You created, care for and will watch over me.

The fragrance of the trees, the song of birds,
The blossoming flowers 'mid the mountain grasses
All whisper to the soul who waits to hear
Saying: 'God passes'.

Nagata
a Christian, Japanese leper

9th April

'O Lord, You are my God . . . a shelter from the
storm . . .'

Isaiah 25:4

Recently I saw two colour slides of the Hebrides I shall never
forget. They were both of the same isolated bay – one a picture of
still, blue peace but the other showed churning, vicious waves
with lightning cutting a leaden sky. It reminded me of life . . . one
moment everything is straightforward and routine, the next a
state of turmoil and the danger of sinking in one of life's storms. It
could be redundancy, being admitted to hospital as an emergency,
finding out my child is taking drugs or my husband prefers other
woman . . . Lord, I must have an anchor for my life: I've got to
hold on to someone who is not just stronger than me, but stronger
than life itself.

We have an anchor that keeps the soul
Steadfast and sure while the billows roll,
Grounded firm and deep in the Saviour's Love.

P. J. Owens

10th April

Jesus asked ' . . . which of these three do you think
was a neighbour to the man who fell into the hands
of robbers?' . . . 'The one who had mercy on him'
Jesus told him, 'Go and do likewise.'

Luke 10:36

Jesus said 'the poor are with you always' and to serve our neighbours God takes and uses some ordinary people to make a most extraordinary contribution to society. In the middle of the last century a young apprentice in a Pawn Shop was upset to see the hand-to-mouth existence of families who were reduced to pawning anything just to buy food. William Booth, the founder of the Salvation Army, whose birthday we remember today, was moved beyond words and into action. The rest of his life was dedicated to helping feed the hungry, clothe the naked and in the name of Jesus, give shelter and love to the homeless and hopeless. Thank you Lord for the work carried on this very day by the Salvation Army amongst the physically, and spiritually needy . . . they are my neighbours too . . . is there anything I can do?

Neighbours are rich folk and poor
Neighbours are black folk and white
Neighbours are nearby and far away:
Jesu, Jesu, fill us with your love
Show us how to serve the neighbours we have from You.

T. S. Colvin
based on a song from N. Ghana

❧

11th April

Jesus said: 'Come to me all you who are weary.'
Matthew 11:28

Saturday – and I'm tired! A real 'end-of-the-week' feeling – I know my tiredness will spill over into impatience, snappy words, waspish answers that I'll hate myself for afterwards. Other people expect me to make allowances and understand when they are tired, but no-one seems to think I may be weary and drained. I feel like a plant that's curling at the edges for want of water. Lord, I know You understand, so I'll take time out to pause, just for a few moments, and come to You for rest . . . soothing, renewing rest.

O love that wilt not let me go
I rest my weary soul in Thee:
I give Thee back the life I owe,
That in Thine ocean depths it's flow
May richer, fuller be.

George Matheson

12th April

Many people spread their cloaks on the road, while others spread branches they had cut from the fields. Those who went on ahead and those who followed shouted: 'Hosanna! Blessed is he who comes in the name of the Lord!'

Mark 11:8

As Jesus entered Jerusalem, He must have known that He was riding into escalating fury and danger. Yet when we read the account of that fateful week it's surprising to see what was recorded: the widow offering her mite, wrangling over second and third wives, mis-use of the Temple, taxes . . . O Lord, it is as though the two thousand years have rolled away . . . we are still wrangling over taxes, divorce; our sights are on the things of this world and the hosannas we sing today will be as short-lived as they were then. Lift me, Lord, as I think of the King of Kings riding into the Kingdom of Eternal Peace. May my symbolic palm branch be the offering of my praise and worship.

Parents, teachers, old and young
All unite to swell the song:
Higher and yet higher rise
Till hosannas reach the skies!

John Henley

13th April

Do not be discouraged, for the Lord your God
will be with you, wherever you go.

Joshua 1:9

The start of another week, Lord, and I take comfort from the promises made to Your servants in the Old Testament which Jesus Himself repeated in the Gospels. I don't know what today holds, but I can make two pretty accurate promises to You. First of all, somewhere along the way, I'm going to let You down but also, promise number two, I will try my best. This day and this week.

Lord, take and use me, for Your purposes and to Your glory.

> *Forth in Thy name, O Lord, I go,*
> *My daily labour to pursue;*
> *Thee, only Thee resolved to know*
> *In all I think, or speak, or do.*

Charles Wesley

14th April

> Jesus asked (the blind man) 'What do you want me
> to do for you?' 'Lord,' he said, 'I want to see'.

Luke 18:41

Too often I turn to Jesus expecting Him to 'do' something for me, and then there is that deflated feeling when things don't turn out as I expect. The great example of Jesus was that He always had time for people, whoever they were, whatever their needs; He not only wanted the blind man to see physically but He wants us all to see spiritually. Frances Jane van Alstyne, that prolific American poet, was blind from the age of six weeks, but that in no way cramped her spirit. As she wrote hymns for her brothers and sisters in Christ whom she could not see, so the direct clarity of her words has drawn many to find Jesus with the eyes of the soul. Lord, I pray that You will make me see with my heart and soul.

> *Perfect submission, perfect delight*
> *Visions of rapture burst on my sight;*
> *Angels descending bring from above*
> *Echoes of mercy, whispers of Love.*

Frances Jane van Alstyne

15th April

> Jesus said 'See that you do not look down on one of
> these little ones . . .'

Matthew 18:10

Jenny and her husband adopted two African orphans, a boy and a girl. As they grew into their teenage years, the girl had problems of identification within a white society which compounded her natural, 'growing-up' problems. Then during one school holiday she helped to look after a little boy with Downes Syndrome and a mini-miracle emerged. With this child, the young girl became patient, caring, protective and responsible – she was genuinely happy to be with a child many of us would find very difficult to cope with. Lord, help me to remember You have a place for all Your children, whatever their handicaps . . . show me that I should look for the goodness in people rather than accept general prejudices and labels. Each one of us has the gift of the love of Jesus to share.

Jesus said: 'Let the little children come to me, and do not hinder them, for the kingdom of heaven belongs to such as these.'
Matthew 19:14

16th April

> Jesus took bread and broke it, gave it to his disciples saying: 'Take it, this is my body.' Then he took the cup, gave thanks, offered it to them, and they all drank from it. 'This is my blood of the covenant, which is poured out for many'.
>
> Mark 14:22

Lord, as I kneel for the bread and the wine, I would be conscious of the symbol of Your broken body and shed blood for the sins of the world – for my sins. I can almost feel the quiet intimacy of that last supper, friends gathered together, honouring the Passover, remembering God's providence in the past. As I remember the past and the goodness of the Lord to me, I take the bread with humble thanksgiving and put my trust in the saving blood of the new covenant.

> *In memory of the Saviour's love*
> *We keep the sacred feast: . . .*
> *By faith we take the bread of life*
> *With which our souls are fed;*
> *The cup is token of His blood*
> *That was for sinners shed.*
>
> Thomas Cotterill

17th April

They brought Jesus to the place called Golgotha
. . . and they crucified Him.

Mark 15:22/24

There is a green hill far away:
    So far, so very far away – in another country, another century,
    another world . . .
    That green hill is mostly out of sight and out of mind:
    Except on Good Friday.
    Today, we commemorate man's hideous violation of God's Son
    With hushed reverence, little understanding, transient remorse.
O dearly, dearly has He loved –
    Loved the unloving, loved the loveless:
And we must love Him too –
    I draw a little closer to the foot of that green hill,
    Close enough to see my Lord hanging on the stark cross
    I mutter and stumble over the words that choke in my throat:
    I believe it was for us . . . for me . . .
    He hung and suffered there.

> *There is a green hill far away*
> *Without a city wall;*
> *Where the Dear Lord was crucified*
> *Who died to save us all.*

Cecil Frances Alexander

18th April

The torrents of destruction overwhelmed me: the
cords of hell coiled around me, the snares of death
confronted me . . .

Psalm 18:5

Jesus the carpenter from Nazareth, the itinerant rabbi, the Son of
God died of a broken heart. At that particular moment when He
was hanging in agony from the cross, life must have been unbearable for Him. The Psalmist depicts that despair, that feeling that
life is not worth living, as death and hell; surely the despair of the
disciples the day after Good Friday must have felt like hell. Lord,
forgive me that I am not as moved as I should be – this account

should take my breath away but I carry on just like any other Saturday. I pray for all today who are going through a personal hell . . . give us all Hope and Love.

God is Love, and he has created men and women to share in His love. He calls us to respond to His love by giving Him our love. If we cannot respond to love then we have already entered hell.

Hugh Montefiore

19th April

He is Risen – He is not here!

Mark 16:6

An empty tomb – Jesus is RISEN. He has destroyed the fear and limitation of death by proving that this life is but one level of understanding . . . it is the greatest miracle mankind has ever been given and it cannot be disproved. Lord, when my eyes are clouded with the cares of the world, or when I tend to look back in time for my faith, show me that Jesus is not in the past, He is no longer in the grave where we could conveniently have gone to pay Him homage, but he is ALIVE: and that very fact must colour all that I think, speak and do.

> *The Lord of Life is risen for aye*
> *Bring flowers of spring to strew His way:*
> *Let all the world rejoice and say*
> *ALLELUIA!!*

C. A. Alington

20th April

The love of money is the root of all kinds of evil

1 Timothy 6:10

Francis Bacon said: Money is like Muck . . . only of any use when it is spread! There is a whimsical truth here, money is no good whatsoever hoarded away in the Bank or Building Society, we cannot take it with us into the next world although many people worship money today above all else. Money on its own is totally useless; only when I exchange money for goods and services is it going to help me yet even then, money will not buy my health, my youth, my peace of mind nor true friendship. Lord, show me ways to use money sensibly so that I am master of it and never let money itself get a hold on my mind, let me recall the words of Jesus 'give to Caesar what is Caesar's and give to God what is God's'.

Take my silver and my gold,
Not a mite would I withhold,
Take my intellect and use
Every power as Thou shalt choose.

Frances Ridley Havergal

21st April

All the people of the land were rejoicing and blow-
ing trumpets, and singers with musical instruments
were leading the praises.

Chronicles 23:13

How flat the day would be without music – how monotonous the radio and television would be with no signature tunes or jingles and what would a football match be without the chanting sup-porters! Thank you Lord for the untold pleasure given by Gospel Groups, singers like Harry Secombe and Cliff Richard, the top quality choirs, orchestras and bands . . . thank you for the way songs hold such special meanings and memories for us. If today is a happy day, I will rejoice with my own personal melody of praise and if there are down patches to cope with, I'll cope more cheer-fully with song in my heart: as the hymn writer Karl Spitta wrote:– 'the Lord gave me the song and I give it back to Him'.

Sing to the Lord a joyful song
Lift up your hearts, your voices raise
To us His gracious gifts belong
To Him our songs of love and praise.

John S. B. Monsell

22nd April

'Take my yoke upon you and learn from me . . .
and you will find rest for your souls.'

Matthew 11:29

To take the yoke Jesus offers is not a guarantee of a cushy number
– it takes a deep-rooted faith to accept 'whatever my lot'. . . . In
the nineteenth century the wife of a Chicago lawyer was crossing
the Atlantic with their four children when the French steam-ship
in which they were travelling collided with another vessel. After
some hours the mother was rescued from the sea but all four
children drowned. Shortly before that fatal journey, the whole
family had attended a Revival Meeting and had given their lives to
Jesus. Two years after the tragedy, despite his terrible loss, the
children's father wrote the words of the hymn below. Lord, give
me Your peace whatever my lot . . .

> *When peace, like a river, attendeth my way,*
> *When sorrows like sea billows roll:*
> *Whatever my lot, Thou hast taught me to know*
> *It is well, it is well, with my soul.*

H. G. Spafford

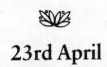

23rd April

As for Titus, he is my partner.

2 Corinthians 8:23

The best form of partnership means co-operation, stability,
strength and loyalty. Dentists, doctors, lawyers, businessmen –
they all join partnerships for their mutual benefit, it makes
common sense as well as good business sense. Yet when it comes
to working in co-operation within a club, sometimes even within
a church, we find we don't see eye to eye, then people get into a
huff and won't take any active part . . . the result of putting self
first and partnership and progress last. O Lord, give me strength
to work in fellowship with people, harmonise our work and
witness together so that our Christ-based partnership will be one

of comfort, growth, tolerance and shared love to the glory of our Saviour Jesus.

> *How can it be Thou heavenly King,*
> *That Thou should'st us to glory bring:*
> *Make slaves the partners of Thy throne,*
> *Decked with a never-fading crown.*

Johann Nitschmann

24th April

> . . . they received the message with great eagerness
> and examined the scriptures every day . . .

Acts 17:11

At the end of a church service there are times when I haven't even reached the door and I've forgotten the passage of scripture which has been read. I begin by concentrating, then all kinds of thoughts take over – I'm going over what happened last week, the need to wash the bedroom curtains, whether there is enough butter in the fridge to last . . . jumbled, tumbling thoughts far removed from eagerly listening to the sacred word of God. O Lord, I need to learn self-discipline, to make sure that every day I make that conscious effort to draw closer to You by reading the scriptures, stories of how a God of Infinite Love cared and guided His men and women in all situations, and be assured that He will do the same for me.

> *For Your holy book, we thank you*
> *And for all who served You well:*
> *Writing, guarding and translating*
> *That its pages might forth tell*
> *All Your love and tender care*
> *For Your people everywhere.*

Ruth Conter

25th April

I will send down showers, – showers of blessing
Ezekiel 34:26

Sometimes I need to be quiet and simply count my blessings – as the song puts it: 'name them one by one'. The blessing of sight to enjoy all the colours of my world; speech, that blessed ability to communicate; I can listen too, to a baby gurgle with pleasure or to interesting programmes on the radio; with my fingers I can feel all different kinds of textures, I can put out my hand in friendship and touch someone in love. I have the blessing of mobility, I can run, dance, walk unaided and stored in my mind are memories of laughter and tenderness. Forgive me Lord that most of the time I take all these blessings for granted – quietly now I hold out my hands for the greatest blessing . . . the gift of Your love.

On all the earth Thy spirit shower
The earth in righteousness renew.

Henry Moore

26th April

I have set my rainbow in the clouds and it will be
the sign of the covenant between me and the earth
Genesis 9:13

I always seem to be worrying about the clouds on my horizon, even though, deep down, I know I'm not the only one to have problems. Perhaps it's only natural to be afraid of the unknown – I dread the thought of moving to another district, the possibility that I may need an operation . . . O me of little faith! Lord, You promised that the rainbow in the sky would be a sign of Your continuing love; help me to face the clouds in my life with calm assurance, after all, they never are so black as I fear . . . and I will lift my heart to see the rainbow of Hope.

We expect a bright tomorrow – All will be well:
Faith can sing through days of sorrow –
        All, all is well.
On our Father's love relying,
Jesus every need supplying,
Then in living or in dying, all must be well!

Mary Peters

27th April

Now a man came up to Jesus and asked: 'Teacher,
what good thing must I do to get eternal life?'

Matthew 19:16

The promising young man who went to Jesus had got the wrong
idea – he was so eager to 'do' something to prove his suitability for
redemption; it's an easy idea to get caught up in . . . that desire to
earn God's love and approval. It is far harder to come to terms
with the fact that there is nothing we can 'do' to winkle our way
into the Kingdom of Heaven. The action has been with God, in the
life and death of Jesus, His action gives me the free gift of eternal
life. Lord, I fall at the foot of the cross to hear the soft command
'Follow me'.

Not what these hands have done
Can save this guilty soul:
Not what this toiling flesh has borne
Can make my spirit whole.
Thy work alone, O Christ
Can ease this weight of sin;
Thy blood alone, O Lamb of God,
Can give me peace within.

Horatius Bonar

28th April

For when I am weak, then I am strong.

2 Corinthians 12:10

Paul never actually said what was wrong with him, but it's plain that he had some physical disorder which made 100% fitness impossible. Weakness gives perspective to our values – suddenly we have to rely on someone else's strength; many people feel bitter and irritated and find it impossible to come to terms with their new and frightening vulnerability. We all are 'frail children of dust'. It's worth remembering that one of the first things a helpless, dependent baby does is to smile! With a Christ-seeking attitude we can learn that physical uncertainty produces spiritual strength just as Paul found. Lord, when my body lets me down, I look for Your strength for my soul – I have nowhere else to turn, keep me from the temptation of self-pity and show me others who are far less fortunate than I.

I am weak, but Thou art strong,
Jesus, keep me from all wrong:
I'll be satisfied as long as I walk,
Let me walk, close with Thee.

Trad. arr M. C. T. Strover

29th April

Peter came to Jesus and asked 'Lord, how many times shall I forgive my brother when he sins against me?'

Matthew 18:21

So many of the questions put to Jesus appear to have been more a seeking after a congratulatory reply than seeking after truth. Peter thought he was being no end of a compassionate man to think of forgiving somebody seven times – that was way beyond what he thought necessary, then Jesus turned his complacency into some realisation of the real cost of being a disciple. God our Father forgives us – we have no right to expect to be able to act any other way than to forgive those who hurt us, cheat us, gossip about us and generally do us down. Lord, I feel like Peter – there is a limit with me too . . . I harbour petty resentments, I don't even try very hard to forgive, there is this awful crust of self-righteousness that I just can't seem to break. Today, I pray with all my heart to get rid of bitterness and unforgiving thoughts . . . help me to know that Your forgiveness is limitless . . .

> *Forgive our sins as we forgive,*
> *You taught us, Lord, to pray:*
> *But You alone can grant us grace*
> *To live the words we say.*
>
> Rosamund E. Herklots

30th April

> Who are you that you fear mortal man, the sons of
> men, who are but grass, that you forget the Lord
> your Maker . . . ?
>
> *Isaiah 51:12*

Let's be honest – some of us are governed by what the neighbours think about us. We set great store by the impression we create; a new car, the holiday abroad, the new three-piece, patio furniture . . . we feel that without these possessions for show, our friends will think we are inadequate, not up to scratch; they are a front we hide behind. Lord, forgive me for behaving in such a silly fashion – of course it doesn't matter a hoot what the neighbours think, what does matter is do I do my best for my family, for You, for others? do I speak gently and without dishonouring Your name? am I a Christian example?

> *Shall I, for fear of feeble man*
> *The Spirit's course in me restrain?*
> *Or, undismayed, in deed and word,*
> *Be a true witness for my Lord?*
>
> Johann Winckler

1st May

Were not our hearts burning within us while He
talked with us . . . ?

Luke 24:32

It always helps to talk about things. Even though we cannot 'see' Jesus, by feeling his nearness, if we explain our problems, generally talk things over with Him, then it's amazing how this helps. After pouring out a knotty situation they will be the more approachable. I don't pretend to understand why God's son should bother to listen to my babblings, but I believe by faith that no-one is outside His concern: the whole gospel is about the depth of caring love, the stories of how Jesus stopped to listen to the humblest of people. Lord, I feel so much better when I have talked to You.

Remember, every morning when you start the day, take a few moments to talk with God. Then, if you spend time in this way, you will say and do the right things in the day, and you will be sure nothing will happen that you cannot face.

George Thomas: Lord Tonypandy

2nd May

They asked, 'What's this wisdom that has been
given Him, that he even does miracles?'

Mark 6:2

People get disillusioned today because, they say, they don't see miracles. Yes, it must have been enthralling to watch Jesus perform miracles, but, if we are prepared to acknowledge them, miracles do still happen today. I'm thinking of the miracle of transplant surgery, the miracles of friendship between nations who were once at war; miracles of communication, forests which have turned into fuel, grass that is turned into milk. Everyday happenings, almost common-place miracles – so ordinary yet so vital. O Lord, my God, there is such a gulf between Your wisdom and mankind's achievements: I praise You for the miracles of love and progress in the world and in my life.

> *How many are the saints of God*
> *Who laboured in this land;*
> *How joyfully they kept the vow*
> *To follow Christ's command:*
> *Their lives were miracles of love*
> *That sinners understand.*

Fred Pratt Green

3rd May

> Then Jesus said, 'The Sabbath was made for man,
> not man for the Sabbath'.
>
> *Mark 2:27*

I've even heard people say they hate Sundays because there is nothing to do! It does seem that the majority of folks make no difference whatsoever on a Sunday and there must be thousands of children growing up not even knowing the significance of Sunday. For me, Sunday is the Lord's Day, the day to gather together to worship, to step aside from the clamour of worldly pressures and get my values realigned. A day of rest and gladness. A day when families get the opportunity to do things together, go visiting relatives, hospitals, parks and so on. Lord, teach me to make my Sunday a really different and Holy day, keep me wise in how I spend the time and may the 'difference' of my Sunday enhance the coming week.

> *O Sabbath rest by Galilee*
> *O calm of hills above;*
> *Where Jesus knelt to share with Thee*
> *The silence of eternity*
> *Interpreted by Love.*

John Greenleaf Whittier

4th May

The woman went back to the town and said to the
people, 'Come, see a man who told me everything I
ever did. Could this be the Christ?'

John 4:28

I wonder how many people were taken to meet Jesus by that
woman? A woman not even given a name, whose life-style left
much to be desired, yet she was the one used to interest her friends
in Jesus Christ. Many years ago a little girl begged her friend to
join the Sunday school and Youth night at their church – today
the girl who issued the invitation has little to do with the church,
but the 'invitee' became a Deaconess and is now a Methodist
minister. None of us can know the way God will use us through a
casual invitation to a friend – Father of all, thank you for those
who first made me interested in Jesus.

Come with joy to meet the Lord,
Forgiven, loved and free;
In awe and wonder to recall
His life laid down for me.

Brian A. Wren

5th May

You are my sheep . . . you are my people, and I am
your God, declares the Sovereign Lord.

Ezekiel 34:31

Not flattering to be compared with sheep but woefully accurate.
One sheep trots off in a certain direction and the entire flock
follows regardless that they haven't the faintest idea where they
are heading . . . just like followers of fashion . . . we all hate to be
any different from the 'crowd'. O Lord, how can I be so miserably
fickle when you are so constant? lead me in Your paths of peace,
righteousness and pleasantness, may I learn to follow Your voice
and not the dictates of friends or fashion.

Souls of men why will ye scatter
Like a crowd of frightened sheep?
Foolish hearts, why will ye wander
From a love so true and deep.

Frederick W. Faber

6th May

Love is patient, love is kind. It does not envy, it does not boast, it is not proud. It is not rude, it is not self-seeking, it is not easily angered, it keeps no record of wrongs.

1 Corinthians 13:4/5

Paul's teaching on love to the first Christians at Corinth is so well known but the more we read it the more we realize how much we have to learn about ourselves, our small way of showing love and of the Love of Jesus which saves the world. O if only we could all love in the way Paul taught, there would be no divorce, no magistrates sitting to hear cases of child abuse, no divisions in families and churches. A perfect world indeed! Lord, I want to learn to love . . . may my only boast today be in Jesus Christ my Saviour and His wonderful Love.

Come to my heart O thou wonderful love,
Come and abide:
Lifting my life till it rises above
Envy and falsehood and pride:
Seeking to be lowly and humble, a learner of Thee.

Robert Walmsley

7th May

If someone forces you to go one mile, go with him two miles.

Matthew 5:41

Surely in this statement Jesus was encouraging his listeners not only to lend a helping hand where necessary but to do so willingly. Nothing is worse than grudging help and there are many times when we act out of duty whilst all the time feeling secretly resentful. Lord, I am ashamed when I think of the attitude of nurses, how they flit from bed to bed, nothing ever too much trouble – I have so much to learn – through this day I would ask for Your guidance so that I will treat people as I would like to be treated myself, with willingness, with justice and friendship.

> *Lord, it is so hard to be caring all the while,*
> *When tempers fray, the tears are close,*
> *And life has lost its style:*
> *Show me I can ride out life's storms*
> *To walk the extra mile.*

Elizabeth Rundle

8th May

And all of the people gave a great shout of praise to the Lord, because the foundation of the house of the Lord was laid. But many of the older priests and Levite family heads, who had seen the former temple, wept aloud . . .

Ezra 3:11/12

The same old story of a new generation praising God in the way most natural and suitable to them, whilst the older generation cannot cope with the changes, so they turn away and grieve. The fundamental truth is that the church is not a building but the worshipping fellowship of believers. It's exciting to see new ventures in faith in small towns and cities too where redundant church buildings are being used for the good of the community, new churches are being built in some areas and in others existing premises are being improved and extended. Lord, help me not to worship a building, but draw me into the active circle of praise where life and witness are the same thing in the community You have set me amongst.

I have a dream of a church (name your church)
  a worshipping church
  a caring church
  an expectant church
  a Biblical church
I have a dream, Lord – Thy will be done.

based on a meditation by John Stott

9th May

I gave you milk, not solid food, for you were not
ready for it. Indeed you are still not ready. You are
still wordly.

1 Corinthians 3:2

The strength and growth of our church depends on the strength
and growth of our faith. All the rallies and special efforts are not
worth a fig if they do nothing for our spiritual growth – and only
God gives the growth. Charles Wesley wrote: O Jesus Christ grow
thou in me, and all things else recede'. To learn about anything
from cookery to taking photographs we have to look at the
instructions and build our way up from simple things to more
complicated efforts; likewise the human body would remain
pretty sickly if we never progressed beyond milk. Even so, there
are those within the Christian fellowship who are reluctant to try
anything beyond the spiritual milk. Forgive me, Lord, if I am one,
if I am trying to live my life with half a foot in the world still –
build me up with the solid food of Your word so that my faith and
church will grow.

  The babes in Christ Thy scriptures feed,
  With milk sufficient for their need,
    The nurture of the Lord.

G. B. Caird

10th May

Jesus said: 'How hard it is for the rich to enter the
Kingdom of God'.

Luke 18:24

A newspaper report carried an unhappy story of a sordid legal
wrangle revolving around a dead millionaire, a discarded woman
and the innocent child of their fleeting affair. The young aristocrat
had money, education, position . . . the world at his feet, and with
all his wealth he shot himself. The mother of his child said
afterwards that his money hadn't made him happy. Jesus offered
the young man eternal life but the cost of losing his wealth and
position was too much and he went away. Lord, I look to money
to make life easier for me – am I deceiving myself? The opportunity is here for me today to follow Jesus or bury my head and
keep my hand firmly on my possessions. I know I can't have it
both ways, Lord . . . guide me.

> *Seek ye first the Kingdom of God*
> *And His righteousness;*
> *And all these things shall be added unto you*
> *Allelu . . . Alleluia!*

Karen Lafferty

11th May

One of the lepers, when he saw he was healed,
came back, praising God.

Luke 17:15

Ten lepers shouted after Jesus because they were too vile and
disease-ridden to go close to Him. They begged to be healed from
the leprosy which had made them outcasts, reviled even by their
families . . . and only one went back to praise God. We find it
hard to believe – yet do we necessarily turn to praise God for all
the good things in our life? Heavenly Father forgive me that my
praise is so tepid, that I am so slow with my thanks . . . Jesus has

cleansed me from the disease of my soul, my whole day should be spent in thanksgiving and praise.

> *Praise God from whom all blessings flow,*
> *Praise Him all creatures here below.*
> *Praise Him above ye heavenly host,*
> *Praise Father, Son and Holy Ghost.*

Thomas Ken

12th May

> Even though I was once a blasphemer and a per-
> secutor and a violent man . . . the grace of our Lord
> was poured out on me.
>
> *1 Timothy 1:13*

In his letter to his young friend Timothy, the apostle Paul spoke honestly of the kind of man he had been before he met Jesus on the road to Damascus. I suppose, Lord, I don't really understand what your transforming love can do in a life . . . give me Your grace to accept that no vile or hateful deed is beyond Your forgiveness and whatever people have done, if they truly repent, they are welcome at the throne of grace . . . My Saviour will speak to prisoners as gently as to priests. Lord, I renounce all that I have been and pray that You will pour out Your grace on me . . . even me.

> *Lord, I can hear of showers of blessing*
> *Thou art scattering, full and free:*
> *Showers the thirsty land refreshing*
> *Let some drops now fall on me . . . even me.*
> *Love of God so pure and changeless*
> *Blood of Christ so rich, so free*
> *Grace of God so strong and boundless*
> *Magnify it all in me.*

Elizabeth Codner

13th May

'Nazareth! Can any good thing come from there?'
Nathaneal asked. 'Come and see,' said Philip.

John 1:46

Brixton! Toxteth! St Paul's! Harmondsworth! Places where people
know despair, tension, resentment, unemployment, racial violence, social deprivation . . . can any good come from there?
Henley! Ascot! Hampstead! Places bathed in affluence, privilege,
prosperity . . . can anything good come from there? A stable – a
busy carpenter's workshop – the bottom of a fishing boat – a
hateful cross of wood . . . what good came from there? Come and
see for yourself – come to Jesus – see how your life in any place can
be used by Him to spread goodness.

> *O let me commend my Saviour to you,*
> *I set to my seal that Jesus is true:*
> *Ye all may find favour who come at His call –*
> *O come to my Saviour – His grace is for all.*

Charles Wesley

14th May

There go the ships . . .

Psalm 104:26

At any sea-port, Dover, Plymouth, Liverpool, Harwich . . . it's
fascinating to watch the ships leave port and slowly disappear
away into the distance. What a vast town confined within a single
ship these days; all the catering, laundry, engine room, skilled
knowledge of the radar operators . . . there go the ships, there go
fathers, sons, husbands, out of sight and over the horizon. Not
only at sea, but those of us on land pass by leaving the briefest of
impressions and away we go over the horizon. We pass those with
family upsets, marriage crises, and we never know, we drift apart
and possibly never meet again. Today, Lord, I pray that my
unwitting example as a 'passing ship' may not be one to dis-
courage or turn someone away from You. In all life's vastness, I
am but one single life . . . yet my life is woven into the fabric of
many other existences: it's exciting, it's challenging, it's God's
world.

O Lord, the sea is so vast and my boat is so small . . .
from a Breton Fisherman's Prayer

15th May

Israel will bud and blossom and fill all the world
with fruit . . .
Isaiah 27:6

Time-lapse photography enables us to glimpse a further miracle in
the line-up of our Divine Creator's design technology and the
opening of a rose bud to full blossom is but one of these miracles.
The slowly maturing flowers are a constant joy in the garden and
we see only too well how quickly flowers die if the buds have been
forced for commercial cutting. I like to think of a day as an
unfolding flower – beginning tight-packed with things to do and
as the hours pass so we open to the atmosphere of life with all its
sun and pollution, some flowers will end the day in a bedraggled
state, buffetted by the wind and rain, whilst others will give
fragrance and pleasure and ultimately bear fruit for the continua-
tion of its type. Lord, help me to bloom and fill my little patch
with the fruits of Your spirit.

> *His purposes will ripen fast*
> *Unfolding every hour:*
> *The bud may have a bitter taste,*
> *But sweet will be the flower.*

William Cowper

16th May

'For this reason a man will leave his father and
mother and be united to his wife, and the two will
become one flesh. So they are no longer two, but
one.'
Matthew 19:5/6

One of the most difficult things to do is to live with someone else –
two independent individuals cannot suddenly merge into a single,

harmonious unit; it takes getting used to, a concentrated effort and deep love. Anyone who keeps themselves first in a relationship dooms it to failure; how we give the cold shoulder to folk who are always one about 'I . . .' this, and 'I . . .' that! Every relationship is a two-way matter, and especially marriage is a blessed teamwork. Lord, You made men and women so different, sometimes frustratingly different in outlook and expectation, but thank You for my partner and help me to cherish our relationship in sickness and in health, for richer for poorer, till death us do part.

O perfect love, all human thought transcending,
Lowly we kneel in prayer before Thy throne,
That theirs may be the love which knows no ending
Whom Thou for evermore dost join in one.
Dorothy F. Gurney

17th May

Remain in me and I will remain in you. No branch
can bear fruit by itself . . . neither can you bear
fruit unless you remain in me.

John 15:4

It is very sad when congregations split because of disagreements on interpretation of God's will. Lord, we can't be all right! Forgive our divisions, our arrogance and general lack of love for each other. We pray for the ability to keep our eyes fixed on Jesus with no side-tracking, no 'ifs' and 'buts' but total commitment to Him. Without Jesus I see that my horizons will never be widened and my faith will be stifled and unproductive . . . help me, Lord, to remain in the True Vine and may the fruit borne of this devotion become a blessing to all.

Live Thou within us, Lord,
Thy mind and will be ours.

John Ellerton

18th May

A cord of three strands is not quickly broken . . .

Ecclesiastes 4:12

With all our various backgrounds, ages, colours, culture, our individual personalities there are few things which unite us in a common experience beyond Home and School. 90% of us has some family or other and, thankfully, 99% of us have been to school. The attitudes that seep into our sub-conscious in our early years stay with us and strongly colour our adult years; but there is a third experience which consolidates the secular and moral laws of right and wrong learned at Home and at School – that is the experience of being within the fellowship of a church. Fewer and fewer people receive any formal teaching about Jesus and so it's not much wonder that more and more people are finding life empty and meaningless. The third strand of faith added to our life's experience means we shall find meaning and purpose and a calm security of being loved with Almighty love. Lord, thank You for my experiences at home, at school and with Your Family, my fellow Christians.

> *Bind us together, Lord*
> *Bind us together with cords that cannot be broken,*
> *Bind us together, Lord,*
> *Bind us together in love.*

B. Gillman

19th May

The whole world sought audience with Solomon to hear the wisdom God had put in his heart. Year after year, everyone who came brought a gift, silver, gold, weapons, spices . . .

1 Kings 10:24/25

A walk around any great palace or historic house open to the public like Osborne House, Hampton Court or Chartwell and there are intimate glimpses of beautiful gifts bestowed from past generations. Some gifts obviously given to curry favour while others remain a gift of real affection. Just like gifts for a Wedding, some are chosen with care and others are pure ostentation. Not many of us will receive gifts like Solomon, horses, baboons, gold and so on, but we all like receiving presents. Lord help me to put thought into gifts I buy, rescue me from the temptation to swank, but above all, I rejoice in receiving Your perfect gift of Jesus my Saviour and my King.

> *Jesus the gift divine I know*
> *The gift divine I ask of Thee;*
> *The truth of my religion prove*
> *By perfect purity and love.*

Charles Wesley

20th May

There is only cursing, lying and murder, stealing and adultery, they break all bounds and bloodshed follows bloodshed.

Hosea 4:2

The lament of the prophet Hosea sounds reminiscent of the front page contents of a Sunday paper. Our hearts hang heavy to read of human nature in the grips of evil; the plight of raw humanity in ever desperate need of redemption. O Lord, in all the sad, war-torn areas of the world, I pray for Your peace; in homes ruined by adultery I pray Your forgiveness and healing; and in miserable, inadequate lives that only produce foul language and violence, I pray for the saving gentleness of Jesus Christ. Divine Physician, how Your children are hurting . . . they are hurting themselves and others . . . bruised and bleeding they reject the good news of the Gospel. Dear God, where is kindness, honesty and hope?

Set your minds on things above, not on earthly things. You must rid yourselves of all such things as these: anger, rage, malice, slander, and filthy language from your lips. Do not lie to each other, since you have taken off your old self and have put on the new self which is being renewed in knowledge of its Creator.

Colossians 3:2

21st May

. . . I put many of the saints in prison (Paul)

Acts 26:10

On this day, two hundred and twenty seven years ago, a truly wonderful 'saint' was born, a saint who was to make all the difference to life in prisons. Elizabeth Gurney was brought up in a loving Quaker family and married a Quaker, changing her name to Fry. A well-to-do lady of her time, she shocked society by visiting women in the stinking Newgate prison. Out of her own money she paid for clean straw, food and materials for them to repair and make clothes. Never mind about society being shocked by her actions, Elizabeth Fry was shocked by the conditions in the prisons and with help from some of her influential friends, very gradually, attitudes and conditions changed for the better. Lord, I give thanks for the untiring example of Elizabeth Fry and all those today who don't shrink from the seamy side of life, but who are motivated by Your love to lift others to a better quality of living.

The real saint is neither a special creature nor a spiritual freak. They do not stand aside wrapped in delightful prayer, feeling pure and agreeable to God. They go right down into the mess and there – radiate God.

Evelyn Underhill

22nd May

'On that day you will realise that I am in my Father and you are in me, and I am in you.'

John 14:20

The Holy Trinity can be a stumbling block to some. A tantalising mystery? . . . double dutch? It's too important to dismiss or devalue just because we can't make sense of the concept of God the Father, Jesus the Son and God the Holy Spirit. As Paul wrote to the Corinthians, at the moment we only see through a glass darkly – or in other words, we don't understand any more than a tadpole can understand that one day it will become a frog and will be able to leap and make noises. Lord, I don't understand but through faith I worship – through trust in the unseen I come closer to 'that day . . . ' promised by Jesus.

'Just as in the sun there are both heat and light, but the light is not heat and the heat not light. But both are one, though in their manifestation they have different forms, so I and the Holy Spirit, proceeding from the Father bring light and heat into the world . . . yet we are not three, but one, just as the sun is but one.'

Sadhu Sundar Singh's vision of
Jesus explaining the Trinity.

23rd May

'My peace I give to you . . . do not let your hearts
be troubled and do not be afraid.'

John 14:22

I shouldn't be afraid, Lord, but I am. Very often it's the silly little things that churn me up . . . I get afraid that friends will find me dowdy, I get afraid the children will find me boring and I lie awake at night troubled because my faith, which once seemed so clear-cut and sure, has stumbled on grey patches of uncertainty. Lord, right now, in this quiet moment I ask for Your peace.

Peace, perfect peace, in this dark world of sin;
The blood of Jesus whispers, 'peace' within.
Peace, perfect peace, our future all unknown?
Jesus we know, and He is on the throne.

E. H. Bickersteth

24th May

Praise be to the God and Father of our Lord Jesus
Christ, who has blessed us in the heavenly realms
with every spiritual blessing in Christ.

Ephesians 1:3

What is praise? It ought to be a spontaneous outburst of joy and
thanksgiving? Forgive me, Lord if I'm ashamed to praise too
loudly in case people think I'm some sort of religious freak – after
all, if I were to win £500,000 I'd be leaping and singing all over the
place, it wouldn't enter my head to be shy about my good fortune.
Today, Lord, help me to leave my inhibitions and reserve behind
me – I have everything to praise You for. With all that I am and all
that through Your grace and to Your glory I may become, I praise
You, honour and adore You.

> To our Lord praise we sing
> Light and Life, friend and King,
> Coming down love to bring
> Pattern for our duty . . . showing God in beauty;
> God is good,
>   God is truth,
>   God is beauty,
>   Praise Him!

Percy Dearmer

25th May

'The wind blows wherever it pleases. You hear its
sound but you cannot tell where it comes from nor
where it is going. So it is with everyone born of the
Spirit.'

John 3:8

Wind! it can cut you in two, make your eyes water, wreak havoc
uprooting trees, it's a danger to high-sided vehicles and caravans
on the motorways; wind generates electricity, powers yachts,
dries washing and aids migrating birds. Invisible wind, yet it's
power and presence is evident for all to see, use and enjoy. Lord, I

pray for the unseen power of Your spirit to be the driving force in my life today and every day.

> *Come as the wind with rushing sound,*
> *And Pentecostal grace . . .*
> *Descend with all Thy gracious powers,*
> *O come, great Spirit, come.*

Andrew Reed

26th May

Cain replied: 'Am I my brother's keeper?'

Genesis 4:9

Lord, it's just hit me how little I truly care that so many in my community do not know Jesus as Lord and Saviour – people who have no anchor for their lives, no faith in life eternal. I do not tremble for them . . . I am not eager to give them a share in how I feel . . . I can see myself like Cain, shrugging off responsibility, or like Jacob, wanting all the blessing for myself and my own. What kind of Christian am I, Lord? Give me a fresh awareness and compassion towards the weaker souls in the neighbourhood – teach me the practical discipline of praying for others to know You and awake in my heart real care for my brothers and sisters in Christ.

> *Rescue the perishing, care for the dying,*
> *Snatch them in pity from sin and the grave:*
> *Weep o'er the erring ones, lift up the fallen,*
> *Tell them of Jesus, the mighty to save.*

Frances Jane van Alstyne.

27th May

Jesus saw a poor widow put in two very small copper coins. 'I tell you the truth,' he said, 'this poor widow has put in more than all the others . . . she has put in all that she had.'

Luke 21:2

On the face of things, I like to contribute to Oxfam, N.S.P.C.C., the Alexander Rose Day, R.N.L.I., The Spastic Society, Earl Haigh Fund and so on as well as all the church connected needs. I like to think that I give generously, and I like others to think I give generously as I expect them to give, but that isn't quite the true picture. The collecting tins get off-loaded with my small change, the left-overs in my purse. And my Lord, too, tends to end up with the left-overs of my time . . . a snatched five minutes of prayer here or a squeezed in Bible reading there . . . the small change from my energies in other directions. Lord, make me ashamed . . . prompt me to give of my best in time, effort, monetary contributions or prayers . . . nothing but my best is acceptable.

> *Saviour, Thy dying love Thou gavest me,*
> *Nor should I aught withhold, my Lord, from Thee.*
> *In love my soul would bow, my heart fulfil its vow.*
> *Some offering bring Thee now, something for Thee.*
>
> Sylvanus D. Phelps

28th May

Speak to one another with psalms, hymns and spiritual songs. Sing and make music in your heart to the Lord.

Ephesians 5:19

When I hear a Salvation Army band playing hymns on the street corner or in the shopping precinct, memories flood into my mind. 'Blessed Assurance' the hymn I first learnt at a Women's Fellowship meeting when I was only eye-level with the table top . . . 'Lead us Heavenly Father, lead us . . . ', a hymn to bring back memories of a friend's wedding. Hymns speak to each of us with their own direct message for our individual needs – help me Lord to use this international language of joy and comfort and let the music in my heart sing to others.

I think that hymns are very underrated things; that some of the most exquisite melodies of modern times are hymns.

Malcolm Muggeridge

29th May

They raise their voices, they shout for joy from the
west they acclaim the Lord's majesty. From the
ends of the earth we hear singing 'Glory to the
Righteous One.'

Isaiah 24:14/16

Majesty – sovereign power – King of Kings and Lord of Lords. All
these phrases and none can begin to convey the power of God our
Creator, the ruler of this world and of our lives. When we think of
the most fantastic and intricate discovery man has made, it pales
into insignificance because man could only discover what God
had already created and designed. Lord, I tend to think so much of
the stories of Jesus, of his humanity and his ministry amongst
men, women and children that my awe and wonder at Your
majesty has unconsciously been dimmed. Forgive me, Lord, today
I will drag my eyes from ground-level and gaze on Your creation
of which I am privileged to be part.

*Part of the spiritual blindness of this age is that we have lost sight
of the majesty of God. We tend to assume that we are the most
important people in the universe, and that God, if He exists at all,
is simply there to serve our requirements. No wonder we know so
little of the true reality of God in our lives.*

David Watson

30th May

God's word is not chained.

2 Timothy 2:9

Paul was chained in prison when he wrote these words to Timothy
– yet the shining truth of that single phrase has been proved in
every generation all over the world. Dictators and Governments
have tried desperately to muzzle evangelists, to eradicate the
Word of God from the hearts and the minds of their people; but
nothing has gagged God's word, no human opposition has ever
managed to chain it. As I read of the growing church in China, in

Africa and South America I am filled with hope and expectancy for the Kingdom . . . Lord, fill me with compassion for the daily expanding family of Your people to whom I belong.

Many experiences in both Old and New Testaments grew out of the imprisonments of God's saints, calling either for God to deliver directly, or to intervene through angels acting in His name. Many today who are captive in the chains of depression can take courage to believe in the prospect of deliverance.

Billy Graham

31st May

Jesus said, 'whoever drinks the water I give him will never thirst. Indeed, the water I give him will become in him a spring of water welling up to eternal life.'

John 4:14

Water means Life. At it's most obvious we think of the oasis surrounded by lush greenery amid the sandy wilderness, and the middle eastern writers of the old testament were far more aware of the vital importance of water than we are today in our tap-turning, water-wasting society. Lord, open my eyes to realise that just as I need water to sustain my physical body, so I need the water of Life for my soul. When life gets dreary and dried-up, and my faith gets dulled by the world's dust, cleanse me . . . refresh me . . . enliven me with the spring of water welling up into eternal life.

Come! and let him who hears say Come! Whoever is thirsty let him come, and whoever wishes, let him take the free gift of the water of life.

Revelations 22:17

1st June

Let us throw off everything that hinders and the sin that so easily entangles, and let us run with perseverance the race marked out for us. Let us fix our eyes on Jesus . . .

Hebrews 12:1/2

I never cease to be amazed at the dedication of athletes. Hour after hour, month after month, pounding along with the same old laborious preparations, sacrificing all kinds of self-indulgent pleasure to achieve peak fitness. From my state of relative flab it's easy to shrug off their efforts as mildly eccentric – but their attitude manages to leave me with a twinge of guilt. The writer to the Hebrews expected Christians to put in just the same training as athletes in our daily lives. O Lord, I am far from dedicated, far from disciplined . . . I'm unfit physically and spiritually – help me to want to be fit and give me Your strength to persevere.

> *Run the straight race through God's good grace,*
> *Lift up thine eyes and seek His face;*
> *Life with its paths before us lies,*
> *Christ is the way, and Christ the prize.*

John S. B. Monsell

2nd June

I tell you, now is the time of God's favour, now is the day of salvation.

2 Corinthians 6:2

I'm never at a loss for reasons why I should put things off – I'm a great one for 'I'll do it later' . . . Years ago I promised to visit a woman in hospital but it was no easy matter to get there, so I kept putting it off. When I finally got to the hospital, she was unconscious and died three days later. Heavenly Father, may I humbly learn by all my mistakes, teach me that there is no time like the present, and that certain opportunities will never arise again. Above all, bring me to realise that Jesus is waiting to bless me, now – this very moment I can receive His salvation . . . and this is something that no one in their right senses should put off.

> *I am coming, Lord,*
> *Coming now to Thee;*
> *Wash me, cleanse me, by the blood*
> *That flowed on Calvary.*

Lewis Hartsough

3rd June

> But while he was still a long way off, his father saw him and was filled with compassion for him; he ran to his son, threw his arms around him and kissed him.
>
> *Luke 15:20*

We speak today of a generation gap as if it is some phenomenon peculiar to this latter part of the twentieth century; whereas, it would appear that every generation in the history of mankind has had a 'gap' – each one has in turn been frustrated and hurt and disgusted by the next. What parent hasn't agonised over the stupidity of a child's rebellion and selfishness and what child hasn't been hopelessly frustrated by parental over-protectiveness, refusal to move with the times . . . the classic situation for most rows. Jesus emphasised that whatever our human failing, God and Father would never turn around and give us the 'that's what you wanted now get on with it' attitude; God is Good, God is Love and when I come to my senses and acknowledge just how much I need Him, then my heavenly Father will run to meet me. Lord, I have been bumptious, self-opinionated and selfish . . . I am sorry.

God deals differently with each of us. He knows no 'typical' case. He seeks us out at a point in our own need and longing and runs down the road to meet us.

Catherine Marshall

4th June

See how the Farmer waits for the land to yield its
valuable crop and how patient he is for the autumn
and spring rains.

James 5:7

Patience! I think I must have been right at the back of the queue
when patience was being given out – I expect everything to work
to my timetable and waiting is met with flinty short-temper. I
ought to be old enough to know that nothing of any value is ever
'instant', life needs care, attention, practice and patience. Instead
of bouncing with exasperation, Lord, today I'll try to direct my
energies into praise . . . the countryside is changing, looking so
beautiful, ripening and maturing. Thank You, Lord, that Your
heavenly timetable makes me wait and pray for the gift of
patience.

> *Praise God for the harvest of farm and of field,*
> *Praise God for the people who gather their yield:*
> *The long hours of labour, the skills of a team,*
> *The patience of science, the power of machine.*
>
> Brian A. Wren

5th June

My God will meet all your needs.

Philippians 4:19

Lord, I do so want to believe these words – forgive me that I
plough into my problems expecting to sort them out myself: then I
feel trapped, I can't see any answer to my need. Then, as a guilty
after-thought, I come praying to You . . . I need tolerance in
dealing with the elderly, kindness with the handicapped, I need
understanding for the lonely and strength to overcome my own
weaknesses. Lord, give me grace to accept Your guidance and the
confidence to know that You, and only You can and will meet all
my needs.

In some way or other the Lord will provide:
It may not be my way,
It may not be thy way,
And yet in His own way
The Lord will provide.

M. W. Cooke

6th June

The seed will grow well, the vine will yield its fruit,
the ground will produce its crop, and the heavens
will drop their dew.

Zechariah 8:12

How lovely the smell of wet grass and hedgerows full of wild honeysuckle, clover, foxgloves and thorn. Lord, how wonderful it is to watch the soft fruits swelling, to see them fresh and moist with dew, to notice the glory of the early summer flower beds and window-boxes and hanging baskets refreshed by an overnight shower. Today, Lord give me joy in the things that I usually take for granted . . . for the sight of a dragon fly, the special greenness of trees, the warmth of the sun, the shape of the clouds – already I feel full of gratitude, praise and reverence for the simple delights that come my way.

Sweet the rain's new fall
Sunlit from Heaven;
Like the first dewfall on the first grass.
Praise for the sweetness of the wet garden,
Sprung in completeness where His feet pass.

Eleanor Farjeon

7th June

I will pour out my Spirit on all people . . . and
everyone who calls on the name of the Lord will be
saved.

Joel 2:28

Reading the story of the life of Jesus, the miracles He performed, His early death and the appearances to 'hundreds' following His resurrection, it's a real eye-opener to continue the story and find that the witnesses to these dramatic, overwhelming events had locked themselves away for fear of the Jews. Today, I come face to face with the power of the Holy Spirit – Jesus lived, died and proved His power over death yet those happenings on their own had not shattered the world – it took the Holy Spirit to make the difference, to turn the world upside down. Lord, on this day of Pentecost, I pray for the power of Your Holy Spirit to pour into my life . . . O come, blest Spirit, come.

When the day of Pentecost came, they were all together in one place. All of them were filled with the Holy Spirit and began to speak in other tongues as the Spirit enabled them . . .

Acts 2:1 – 4

8th June

Men came bringing a paralytic; they made an opening in the roof, lowered the bed the paralysed man was lying on . . .

Mark 2:4

Bed is the most beautiful place to be – unless you've got to be there! When the alarm goes, the bed is twenty times more snug than when we climbed in, there is a comforting, warm, enfolded feeling that we are so loathed to leave. How strange that the self same bed can turn into a stale, narrow prison for those, like the man unceremoniously taken to Jesus, who are unable to leave their beds. Lord, thank You for my comfortable bed and my health – and if one day I should have to spend long periods in bed, I pray that You will be my help and my strength . . . during those long, lonely hours take my mind away from myself where through the radio, book or television, I can again 'walk' I can still communicate and live with my mind, heart and soul.

O God, you are my God,
Earnestly I seek You;
On my bed I remember You
I think of You through the watches of the night
Because You are my help;
I stay close to You . . .

Psalm 63 1/6/8

9th June

Jesus said, 'You are my friends . . .'

John 15:14

Jesus didn't call his disciples servants, He called them and treated them as friends – much to the disgust of the Pharisees who disparagingly termed Him 'friend of sinners!' Jesus, the Son of God did not keep himself aloof and separate from people, he mixed and mingled and those who follow His commands and example must also mix and mingle without preference. Lord, I want to be called Your friend too, help me not to feel superior, help me not to pre-judge people, but in all I do, to behave as a friend.

> *Friend who never fails or grieves us –*
> *Faithful, tender, constant, kind!*
> *Friend who at all times receives us,*
> *Friend who came the lost to find,*
> *Sorrow soothing, joys enhancing,*
> *Loving until life shall end –*
> *Then conferring bliss entrancing*
> *Still in Heaven, the sinner's Friend.*

Newman Hall

10th June

Then will the eyes of the blind be opened and the
ears of the deaf unstopped . . .

Isaiah 35:5

In the great Jewish hope of the glorious Day of the Lord when the
world as it is known will be turned upside down, they believed
that all the physical afflictions that spoil our lives, will be no more.
An idyllic kingdom of justice, peace, brotherhood and physical
and political freedom . . . how we all long for such a world! Lord,
I can't really relate to such international ideals, such grand and
far-off dreams . . . more immediate to me are my surroundings
and the people and things within my reach, on whom I depend or
who depend on me. I pray for those today who are learning to
cope with blindness . . . for those living in a silent world . . . their
cheerfulness and abilities are astounding and put me to shame,
they humble me . . . they have their part to play perhaps just in
prodding me into gratitude.

> *My hands are numb and broken,*
> * I am blind*
> *And I can neither feel nor see*
> *My little pot of violets:*
> *So I bend to kiss the wee, sweet flowers*
> *That mean so much to me.*

Mumei
Japanese Christian leper

11th June

For this God is our God for ever and ever; He will
be our Guide.

Psalm 48:14

'Have you been inside St Andrew's church?' . . . 'Oh, yes,' I
replied. 'Did you see the engraving on the window-ledge? . . . Did
you notice the slate floor . . . ? Did you see the family tomb in the
corner? . . . ' I felt blank – only a few months before I had gone
around the church and now it was as if I'd not taken notice of
anything. Yes, I should have bought a guide book, but I was only
on a short visit . . . I thought I would see all that was necessary.
How often we treat the Bible like a tourist's guide book and

relying upon ourselves we miss the most obvious promises from God. Lord, show me the wisdom in studying Your word to guide me through the sometimes intricate maze of my days, I believe Your promise that You will be with me, before me, behind me and within me, for ever and ever.

> *O Jesus I have promised to serve Thee to the end,*
> *Be Thou for ever near me, my master and my friend.*
> *I shall not fear the battle if Thou art by my side,*
> *Nor wander from the pathway if Thou wilt be my guide.*
>
> J. E. Bode

12th June

. . . What is your life?

James 4:14

For the past two decades and more, television viewers sat enthralled by the more familiar phrase 'This is your life!' In a way the two are distinctly linked: This is your life . . . the here and now. We all have airy-fairy dreams, flights of fancy which never materialize but sometimes get out of hand in that we waste the here and now. What is your life? what have you done? what are you doing? if you died tonight how would people remember you? Lord, help me not to be afraid to think seriously about my life – I don't want to waste what you have given me; this is my life, the only life I have, and what I am I dedicate to Your service in Jesus Christ.

> *Take my life and let it be*
> *Consecrated, Lord, to Thee; . . .*
> *Take myself, and I will be,*
> *Ever, only, all for Thee.*
>
> Frances Ridley Havergal

13th June

This is what the Lord says: I am the first and I am
the last, apart from me there is no God.

Isaiah 44:6

The prophet here wrote in a climate of multiple tribes and multiple gods and he was urging the wayward Israelites in Exile, not to be influenced by the other gods around them, but to hold fast to the faith of their fathers in the one true God. Ancient tribes and cultures have all worshipped some kind of superior 'power', be it the moon, sun, totem pole or what have you, there is that instinct deep within every soul that there is 'something' we can't understand or control – the Athenians in Paul's day called it the Unknown god. Lord, I believe that You are the God who is able to be known by us all, by any who will come to You – I believe You are God of this world and all worlds and that one day, You will come again . . . may I be prepared.

Behold, I am coming soon! My reward is with me and I will give to everyone according to what he has done. I am the Alpha and the Omega, the first and the last, the beginning and the end.

Revelation 22:12/13

14th June

Suppose a woman has 10 silver coins, and loses
one. Does she not light a lamp, sweep the house
and seek carefully until she finds it?

Luke 15:8

Have you ever lost something valuable? A wedding ring perhaps, or a watch . . . a handbag with cheque book, card et al? We've all experienced that hot and cold sweat of panic, the hastily retraced steps and then . . . oh, the relief, the spontaneous joy of finding what was lost. Is that really the feeling in Heaven when a sinner is 'found' by God? I hardly dare believe that anyone would be bothered whether I was lost or found . . . Lord, Your love is so wonderful, so all embracing . . . I long to be 'found' and to be brought into the light and joy of Your rejoicing love.

Father, who in Jesus found us
God whose love is all around us
Who to freedom new unbound us
Keep our hearts with joy aflame.

Fred Kaan

15th June

Your sons and daughters will prophesy, your old
men will dream dreams and your young men will
see visions . . .

Joel 2:28

The Bible tells us that when the Spirit of God takes hold of lives
they long for better things, to change the hearts and ways of men,
to fight for justice and equality, to turn dreams into reality to the
glory of God. Amazing things have been accomplished because of
a small hope, a dream has been spirit-transformed . . . Lord, give
me the openness of heart to grasp a vision of what Your kingdom
might be if only men and women looked to You . . . I pray for a
vision of healed family rifts, I dream of an end to racial tension,
religious dissent and wrangle, I put my faith in the prophesy that
one day, these dreams will all come true.

I have a dream . . .

Martin Luther King

16th June

Jesus said, 'I am the light of the world. Whoever
follows Me will never walk in darkness, but will
have the light of life.'

John 8:12

One hundred and fifty-four years ago today a young clergyman
on his way home to England, was becalmed in the Mediterranean
Sea between Corsica and Sardinia. To pass away the time he

wrote poetry, including verses which are now sung by Christians all over the world who look to Jesus as the light of their lives. Lord, some of us may feel becalmed today, be our direction . . . and in the long days of June light, draw me closer, lead me along life's road bathed in the radiance of Christ's love.

Lead kindly light, amid the encircling gloom,
*   Lead Thou me on:*
The night is dark, and I am far from home,
*   Lead Thou me on;*
Keep Thou my feet, I do not ask to see
The distant scene, one step enough for me.

John Henry Newman

17th June

Even the stork in the sky knows her appointed seasons, and the dove, the swallow and the thrush observe the time of their migration.

Jeremiah 8:7

It's baffling to look at a little swallow and realise that it has flown thousands of miles since last summer and yet here it is back again to nest in the same barn . . . incredible . . . such a breath-taking constancy – man's world can be in all sorts of upheaval but God's world carries on secure and unchanging. There is the old country saying that when swallows fly high the weather will be good but when they skim the ground it's going to be wet, the country saying or not, the swallow seems to have more wisdom than human weather forecasters. Thank you, Lord for these small birds which visit each year and thank you for all the birds that throughout the year, give me such pleasure.

I love to watch the swallow skim
The river in his flight . . .

Edward J. Brailsford

18th June

I the Lord do not change.

Malachi 3:6

So much around me is changing. New estates, new stores, traffic diversions, one-way systems – the neighbours have moved and the doctor is retiring. It's even changing at church . . . friends have gone, there are people I don't know and changes in the services I don't like. The children are changing too, growing up wrapped in their own world of computers and pop-star videos where I just don't belong. I'm changing . . . ageing . . . and I find it all rather frightening and bewildering. Lord, where can I find security and peace of mind in this ever changing scene?

> *Change and decay in all around I see:*
> *O Thou who changest not, abide with me.*
>
> Henry Francis Lyte

19th June

> Noah, a man of the soil, proceeded to plant a vineyard when he drank some of its wine he became drunk and lay uncovered in his tent.
>
> *Genesis 9:20*

The Bible honestly portrays God's servants complete with all their warts. Noah, the righteous, God-fearing man who had obeyed the voice of God in the face of ridicule, who had kept his faith in the panic of the rising flood waters . . . dear old Noah was still so human he went and got drunk – blotto! It teaches us how perilously easy it is to sink to the daftest level of behaviour and do things which could ruin our lives and those around us. Lord God, I need help – temptation is veiled in pleasure . . . I pray for families who have been broken because of the effects of alcohol, a drunken driver, it is so easy to fall into sin, all too easy and it is so hard to accept my weakness and lean on my Lord for strength and safety.

Be very careful then how you live . . . do not get drunk on wine, which leads to debauchery. Instead be filled with the Spirit.
Ephesians 5:15/18

20th June

His glory covered the heavens and his praise filled the earth: His splendour was like the sunrise.

Habakkuk 3:3/4

One morning I stood on an empty railway platform waiting for the 6.08 train. The sky was an almost opaque blue, the air smelt green and crisp and bird-song was the only noise to pierce the dawn. As the sun rose I could only think of God's glory streaming from Heaven to our Earth and embracing it with warmth, light and life. All the dark mysteries of night melt in the sun's rays and life is easier to face in the light of day. O Lord, God of Heaven and Earth and Sky, lift me from the darkness of my sin into the bright morning hope in Your risen Son.

> *Sun of my soul Thou Saviour dear,*
> *It is not night if Thou be near:*
> *O may no earth-born cloud arise*
> *To hide Thee from Thy servant's eyes.*

John Keble

21st June

Your love has given me great joy and encouragement.

Philemon 7

We can never underestimate how much our prayers and thoughts mean to others. It's good to mention friends by name in the moments of intercession during worship . . . it gives people a sense of encouragement and belonging. Many are unable to attend worship through ill-health, age, frailty, dependent relatives or shift work and it truly enriches the bonds of fellowship with them to make certain they know they have not been forgotten. Lord, I bring to You those known to me who need the support of prayer and in thankfulness I remember those who over the years have prayed for, supported and encouraged me.

> *Help us to help each other, Lord*
> *Each other's cross to bear:*
> *Let each his friendly aid afford*
> *And feel his brother's care.*

Charles Wesley

22nd June

One of the synagogue rulers, named Jairus, fell at
Jesus' feet and pleaded . . . 'My little daughter is
dying – please come and put your hands on her so
that she will be healed and live.'

Mark 5:22

Today Lord, I pray for the children who lie in hospital beds,
children living in schools for special handicaps and children loved
and cared for at home. My prayers are for the anxious, helpless
parents as they watch their child deteriorate or fail to grasp the
basic forms of communication. Heavenly Father, we plead more
earnestly for our children than ever for ourselves and we feel so
heart-broken at the suffering endured by innocent young lives . . .
in Your mercy support families in their time of trial . . . perhaps
prayer will not be answered in the way expected, but Lord, we
know that all things will work together for good for those who
truly love You.

*Father, thank you for all the good gifts you have given to Everett
Lee and to us. Thank you for answering our prayers for him to be
made completely whole. Please give us the comfort we need right
now.*

Everett Payton's prayer on the death of
his handicapped son

23rd June

God made the earth by his power, he formed the
World by his wisdom and stretched out the
heavens by his understanding.

Jeremiah 10:12

An electrical power cut plunges us into confusion – no washing
machine, no cleaner, no shaver, no hair drier . . . we rely on
power so much that we don't notice until it's not there! There are
all sorts of power today, nuclear power, power behind rockets,

power of wind and waves the power of the resurrection – there is the power I mumble about in the Family Prayer, 'for thine is the kingdom and the power and the glory . . . ' all this power: I don't understand it, it's all far beyond me, even so I am bold enough to ask for the power of Your Holy Spirit.

Lord my mind is so small
I can't comprehend the vastness, the power that are Yours,
Your hand bringing together the atoms, energy,
Your hand bringing order out of chaos.
Lord of history
Lord of the future
I need You.

Eddie Askew

24th June

Jesus often withdrew to lonely places and prayed.
Luke 5:16

If Jesus needed to get away from the hurly-burly then how much more should we make the effort to take time away from the telephone, the ironing, the demands of family and retreat somewhere quietly to pray. Lord, I need to breath, just to relax, to bring you the anxieties the large and small irritations – I need to share hopes and joys – in the quietness take my prayer . . . enfold my life so that when I return to the routine I can face the noise, the pressure and the mundane with serenity and a smile.

Prayer is – 'a silence and a shouting' a burst of praise digging deep down into loneliness, into me, Loving. Abandonment to despair, a soaring to heights which can be only ecstacy, dull plodding in the greyness of mediocre being, laziness, boredom, resentment.'
Michael Hollings and Etta Gullick

25th June

Your strength will equal your days.
Deuteronomy 33:25

However beautiful the day, there are times when we just get to the end of our tether . . . it's reassuring to know that even the most well-ordered and prosperous-looking life is not immune from the occasional hiccup. Life holds so many examples of men and women whose faith sees them through difficulties; the Bible is packed with stories where ordinary lives have been strengthened by the Lord God . . . it's nothing new yet it's hard to rely totally on the Lord to do the same thing for us. Lord, how sickly my faith at times, show me that I have nothing to fear with You beside me.

> *For this and only this I pray*
> *Strength for today, just for today.*
> *Strength for each trial and task,*
> *What more, my Father should I ask?*
> *Just as I need it, day by day,*
> *Strength for my weakness, this I pray.*

E. E. Rexford

26th June

> Jesus was telling a parable: 'when the wheat sprouted and formed heads then the weeds also appeared.'
>
> *Matthew 13:26*

Whatever seed we sow, it may be grass seed, flower or vegetable seeds, but as the first tiny shoots push through the earth – lo and behold – weeds have infiltrated to make life exasperating for farmers and for gardeners: to rub salt into the wound it's usually the weeds which look the stronger too! Jesus used a commonplace analogy because each person can link it to their own lives . . . we sow the best of intentions yet we are always plagued by the weeds of discord . . . somebody always gets their nose put out of joint. As I look at my life, Lord, I'm dismayed by all the weeds – where have they come from?

> *All the world is God's own field*
> *Fruit unto His praise to yield;*
> *Wheat and tares together sown*
> *Unto joy or sorrow grown.*

Henry Alford

27th June

The Lord is good – a refuge in time of trouble.

Nahum 1:7

A television programme on wild-life showed rare and beautiful film of fox cubs playing together in a copse . . . frisking and carefree. Suddenly a noise alarmed them and like greased lightning all the cubs had disappeared back to the vixen's side. They'd been content to wander and explore to play and ignore their mother until trouble threatened – then they knew exactly where to go. It's the same with me, Lord, I know you are good but I too am content to stray off doing what amuses me until I need you – then I come running. Don't let me stray too far in case, one day I lose my way 'home'.

> *Other refuge have I none,*
> *Hangs my helpless soul on Thee:*
> *Leave, ah! leave me not alone*
> *Still support and comfort me.*

Charles Wesley

28th June

The sun has one kind of splendour, the moon
another and the stars another.

1 Corinthians 15:41

One of my favourite moments is to stand at the backdoor gazing up at the night sky. The longer I look, my eyes get accustomed to the sky and more and more stars become visible. The moon hangs over the world changing from a rich orange gold into brilliant silver as it rises through the summer night. Just to think I am part of this vast and fabulous universe . . . just as each star belongs to its own constellation and the moon has its set phases, so there is a pattern marked out for my life. Lord, I'm lost in wonder, love and silent praise.

> *Jesus is Lord: creations voice proclaims it*
> *For by his power each tree and flower was planned and made;*
> *Jesus is Lord, the universe declares it*
> *Sun, moon and stars in heaven cry: Jesus is Lord.*

David J. Monsell

29th June

For as in Adam all die, so in Christ all will be made
alive!

1 Corinthians 15:22

To lovers of Handel's oratorio 'Messiah', the words of Paul take on an extra thrill in the way the music is written . . . so in Christ all will be made alive . . . Alive in Christ! What a promise – what a reality! Yet still the majority of people are frightened to die; well, nobody actually wants to die, not even Jesus wanted to die, but through Him as the hymn writer put it 'by death I shall escape from death and life eternal gain'. Lord, help me to mean it when I say I'm not afraid of death, surround me with Your calm and the certainty that because Jesus has broken the terrors of death He will bring me into new life in the eternity of His love. Lord, I pray for all those I have loved and who have died . . . thank You that now Christ has made them alive too.

Jesus said: 'even Moses showed that the dead rise, for he calls the Lord, "the God of Abraham, and the God of Isaac and the God of Jacob". He is not the God of the dead, but of the living, for to Him, all are alive.'

Luke 20:37

30th June

Pray continually, give thanks in all circumstances.

1 Thessalonians 5:17

Although Martin Rinkart wrote more than 40 hymns, there is one which has become an 'institution'. It shines with the certainty of faith honed by rough experiences – he was a pastor in a German city besieged in the Thirty Years War; he performed the funeral service for literally thousands who died there from wounds, disease and famine. His first wife died in that city and Martin's tireless work amid the hideous conditions physically wore him out. But in spite of all he suffered, and the suffering all around him, this pastor continued to thank God. Quietly, Lord, I ask myself could I? Do I? And if not, why not? Today I'll make sure I remember to be grateful in all circumstances.

Now thank we all our God
With hearts and hands and voices . . .
Who from our mother's arms hath blessed us on our way,
With countless gifts of love, and still is ours today.

Martin Rinkart

1st July

In the course of my life He broke my strength, He
cut short my days.

Psalm 102:23

Every day hundreds of tragic accidents change people's lives forever. They happen everywhere, on the road going to school, in the home decorating, or holiday or playing sport – suddenly, in a heart-stopping second a life is cut down. Gaiety and independence turns to crippling pain and fear. Yet we never think it is going to happen to us . . . Lord, I ask for patience and Your grace if a time should come when my physical strength is broken . . . keep me cheerful and grateful for nursing, guard my mind from bitterness, don't let me thrash about blaming people but lead me to be joined to the will of Jesus Christ, I will not be able to understand, but I must be able to keep my faith, my hope and my compassion.

Before almost any good thing can be achieved in our lives we need
to be broken. This involves losing our pride, bowing our wills and
seeing our sinful selves for who we really are.

Joni Eareckson

2nd July

In Joppa there was a disciple named Tabitha who
was always doing good and helping the poor.

Acts 9:36

Tabitha, or Dorcas, was just an ordinary woman yet because of her dedication to Jesus she became an extraordinary example. With a few words her life has been immortalised to every generation . . . she will for ever be remembered because she was a good and kind person. Another woman, about whom very little is generally known, yet whose influence will stand out through the centuries, is the wife of John Bunyan. She married a hell-raiser, yet through her continuous prayers and the work of the Holy Spirit John Bunyan was converted – totally transformed and with his wife's help he found a faith so strong that all who read his Pilgrim's Progress are touched by it. Lord, what better thing could I do today than to be kind, good and pray for someone to find you.

> *In sickness, sorrow, want or care,*
> *Whate'er it be, 'tis ours to share;*
> *May we, where help is needed, There*
> *Give help as unto Thee.*

Godfrey Thring

3rd July

Noah removed the covering from the Ark and saw
that the surface of the ground was dry.

Genesis 8:13

In this predominantly holiday month we all look for the ground to be dry – we want warmth and sunshine for ourselves, for those going on holiday, to dry the clothes, dry the hay, ripen cereal crops and so that we can open all the windows to let in lovely, dry fresh air. There are times when we need to throw open the windows of our minds to let the breath of the Spirit refresh us, dry up our tears and bring us into the sunshine of Jesus' face. Lord, whatever today holds, I pray for perseverance when things don't go right and I ask for the ability to share the warmth I feel inside with those whose days are difficult and colourless.

> *When my work seems hard and dry*
> *May I press on cheerily . . .*

John Page Hopps

4th July

Jesus said: 'see how the lilies of the field grow . . .'

Matthew 6:28

Getting down on hands and knees to trim the edge of the lawn is an excellent way to take an eye-level view of individual blooms – the intricate marking, the vibrant colours, scent, shape . . . exquisite and individually perfect. Then, to see the wonder of flowers on a grander scale, a visit to a Flower and Vegetable Show or the floral art exhibitions engulfs us in a sea of beauty. Jesus told his listeners that no man-made beauty could match the precision and splendour of a natural, God-made lily. Lord, thank You for all these wonderful flowers, from the tiniest to the most flamboyant . . . the pleasure they give crosses all boundaries of language and culture . . . they bloom and grow to remind us all of Your glory.

Here, Lord, we offer Thee all that is fairest,
Bloom from the garden and flowers from the field . . .

Abel. G. W. Blunt

5th July

However, if you suffer as a Christian do not be ashamed, but praise God that you bear His name.

1 Peter 4:16

Sunday morning – neighbours cleaning the car, mowing the lawn or still in bed . . . one can feel out of step with the world at large by going to church. I ask myself, Lord, why should I be ashamed to go to church . . . where do I really stand? Do I enjoy jokes against the church and clergy . . . on the beach would I get up and join in the choruses of a mission group or would I keep well away – Lord, I don't suffer in any way at all to be a Christian, I pray today for my brothers and sisters in countries where they do suffer for bearing Your name; please forgive me my unease and embarrassment fill my heart with joy and the courage of my convictions, may my boast be in Jesus Christ my Lord.

I am not ashamed to own my Lord.

Isaac Watts

6th July

Light is sweet, and it pleases the eyes to see the sun.
Ecclesiastes 1:7

Isn't it funny how the sunshine can make us feel better? Today I walked along the seashore in bright sunshine – the water sparkled and danced . . . children splashed and laughed with uninhibited pleasure – life was good. The whole world seemed a brighter place. Jesus speaks of the people of God shining like the sun; how lovely to be like that – to inject relationships with warmth, to be a sunny personality who can make someone else feel better. O Lord, help me to find the reality of the old Sankey hymn:

> *There is sunshine in my soul today*
> *More glorious and bright*
> *Than glows in any earthly sky*
> *For Jesus is my light!*

E. E. Hewitt

7th July

Do not forget to entertain strangers for by so doing some people have entertained angels without knowing it.
Hebrews 13:2

Who is a stranger? I like to think that a stranger is a friend as yet unknown. Impression can be misleading when we first meet someone and the early Christians were warned about jumping to conclusions about people's clothes and looks, and also they had to be told 'don't forget to do good'. Life is no different now, we still need reminding or we become becalmed in indifference to the needs around us. Lord, You were a stranger once . . . a stranger whom the crowds flocked to see – a novelty – a dynamic teacher people wanted to get to know; I want to know You more day by day. In Your strength, Lord, teach me to be fair and sympathetic towards strangers.

> *In fancy I stood by the shore one day,*
> *Of the beautiful murmering sea;*
> *I saw the great crowds as they thronged the way*
> *Of the Stranger of Galilee.*

C. H. Morris

8th July

The Lord appeared to Abraham . . . while he was sitting at the entrance to his tent in the heat of the day.

Genesis 18:1

Camping is a wonderfully relaxing activity – in a tent one can get away from clocks, timetables, lorry fumes, bus queues, the stuffiness of central heating . . . there is the peace of nature in a tent. There is time to watch the bugs and beetles trundle through the blades of grass . . . time to hear grasshoppers and birds . . . to smell the cool, dark earth. No wonder Abraham was receptive to God as he sat at the entrance to his tent. Lord, I'm so used to carpets and comfy chairs, I've forgotten the simple, natural things . . . I want to get away from man-made things and come into Your presence joyfully praising the God of Abraham, the God of Isaac and of Jacob, the Lord of all creation.

> *Hail Father, Son and Holy Ghost,*
> *Hail Abraham's God, and mine,*
> *All might and majesty are thine,*
> *And endless praise.*

Thomas Olivers

9th July

Be still before the Lord and wait patiently for Him.

Psalm 37:7

O Lord, I find it so hard to 'wait' – life is programmed for immediate solutions, instant results and I find waiting in prayer, waiting for comfort, waiting to know Your will beyond me. I know it's silly and there are so many things we happily wait for – a child's first words, for a guide dog to be trained, these things we accept gladly are worth waiting for. But I can't keep rushing around, Lord, I must be still for a while, I must wait to be renewed by Your Spirit or I shall burn up before the end of the day . . . I pray for my faith to grow into maturity that I may wait for my Lord contentedly and with a peaceful frame of mind.

Those who wait upon the Lord will renew their strength.

Isaiah 40:31

10th July

The Lord said to Moses, 'Come up to me on the mountain and stay here.'

Exodus 24:12

Mountains are magnetic once you've tried them, they draw people back to experience that oneness between man and infinity. Mountains symbolise strength and time is lost; Lord, in the rugged grandeur of mountains we too can feel like Moses, away from the clamour of responsibilities, breathing deeply the pure air and drawing us closer to spiritual realities. What a wonderful world – full of mountains and valleys, of rivers and forests, there is scenery for all to enjoy – I want to thank you, Lord, for the places I can visit close to home which bring praise to my lips.

Rock and highland,
Wood and island,
Crag, where eagle's pride has soared:
Mighty mountains, purple-breasted,
Peaks cloud-clearing, snowy-crested,
Praise ye, praise ye God the Lord.

John Stuart Blackie

11th July

For You make me glad by Your deeds, O Lord. I
sing for joy at the work of Your hands.

Psalm 92:4

Isaac Watts wrote about the wonders of the Lord, wherever he
happened to look and that's how I want to be today. All around
me the goodness of the Lord makes me glad, gives a new zip to
familiar surroundings. I will rejoice and be glad at the sight of
fresh vegetables and fruit, at the variety of both in the super-
market freezers and in the tins on the rows and rows of shelves. I
will enjoy people's gardens as I pass by and the trees in the park.
Lord, this is another new day . . . lift my life to gladness.

I will enter His gates with thanksgiving in my heart,
I will enter His courts with praise,
I will say this is the day that the Lord has made,
I will rejoice for He has made me glad.

Anon

12th July

We finally gave up all hope of being saved . . .

Acts 27:20

It must be terrifying beyond belief to be involved in a collision, a capsize or indeed any disaster at sea and to give up hope that anyone will be rescued. On Sea Sunday, it's good to remember the million plus merchant seamen and fishermen worldwide, whose daily job is to supply the markets with all the foodstuffs we have come to expect. It's also timely to stop and thank God for all the Lifeboat crews, coastguards, search and rescue helicopter pilots who risk their own lives to save strangers when they get into trouble at sea. Lord, in their selflessness, I sense the sacrifice of the Son of Man who gave His life to save the world.

> *Eternal Father, strong to save*
> *Whose arm doth bind the restless wave;*
> *O hear us, when we cry to Thee*
> *For those in peril on the sea.*

William Whiting

13th July

Jesus said: 'There were many widows in Israel in Elijah's time, yet Elijah was not sent to any of them, but to a widow in Zarapheth.'

Luke 4:25

Jesus was using the illustration of Elijah to underline to His contemporaries that a prophet never receives the acknowledgement due to him from his own people. He may also have been implying the universal appeal of His gospel – if rejected by His own, the Jews, then the welcome to the Kingdom of God would be to all races, colours, creeds – for anyone who could approach Jesus as Lord. Forgive me, Lord, that I am guilty of dismissing Your messengers and help me today to put all my trust in You – I know the stories of others trusting and I know You never let them down . . . Have mercy on me and guide me in Your truth.

The woman said to Elijah: 'Now I know that you are a man of God and the word of the Lord from your mouth is the truth.'

1 Kings 17:24

14th July

Swing the sickle for the harvest is ripe.

Joel 3:13

An old Cornish farmer was known to go into his kitchen after the day's work and sigh: 'Oh, well, what isn't done today will be done tomorrow!' His mother, in her eighties, would snap back 'What isn't done today ought to have been done yesterday!' At this time of year when there are so many obvious jobs to be done, farmers working all hours bringing in hay and sillage, jobs in the garden, in the house and on the car, Lord show me that life is always easier when work is shared, completed with willing, friendly hands . . . and when I'm tempted to put things off until tomorrow, teach me the discipline of tackling a job right now, when I am able and everything is ready. That way, Lord, I will accomplish more than I expected in daily and in spiritual things.

Leave not for tomorrow the work of today,
The moments are precious, then why should we stay –
The Master is calling again and again,
'Go thrust in the sickle and gather the grain'.

Fanny J. Crosby

15th July

'Therefore go and make disciples of all nations, baptising them in the name of the Father and of the Son, and of the Holy Spirit and teaching them to obey everything I have commanded you.'

Matthew 28:19

What a daunting task to go out into all the world – to live in a foreign culture, learn another language just to take the love of Jesus to others. Lord, I remember today those missionaries whom I know personally, and indeed for all those who have gone to serve You overseas. When I think of their long hours and heartaches it makes me see how little I am prepared to give You. As I pray for missionaries may their witness, commitment and compassion move me towards a greater awareness of the church world-wide . . . Lord, I am ashamed that I'm so bound up with my self, my family, my interests . . . there is little room for others . . . and less understanding of Your great command.

> *Baptize the nations: far and nigh*
> *The triumphs of the cross record;*
> *The name of Jesus glorify*
> *Till all the earth shall call Him Lord.*
>
> James Montgomery

16th July

'I am the Lord your God . . . You shall have no
other gods before me.'

Exodus 20:2/3

There is no substitute for God – there is no excuse for the list of things and people we place before God – no excuse for substituting horoscopes for faith, or relying on the cushion of a fat bank balance to solve all our worries. There is no drug, no club, association or possession which will satisfy our minds and souls in place of God. We have been told, we have been warned and in the life of Jesus we have been shown how God must come first. Lord, I do try, but I don't seem to do very well . . . help me.

None other Lamb, none other Name,
None other hope in heaven or earth or sea;
None other hiding-place for guilt and shame,
None beside Thee.

Christina Georgina Rossetti

17th July

You shall not make yourself an idol in the form of
anything in heaven above or in the earth below.

Exodus 20:4

When I was very young I had a huge two-page colour picture of my
screen idol held by drawing pins in the lid of my school desk. Over
the years there have been other idols and I don't have to look far to
see others with their particular idols: the golf club, the caravan,
the video and so forth. Idols are of our own making which
inevitably let us down. The Israelites made a golden calf; ancient
tribes have created all sorts of magical and weird idols for themselves but we, in our so-called civilized society who ought to know
better, find out, if we are honest, that we look for the easy
gratification of man-made gods which do not stretch us or face us
with any more dilemma. Lord, I need to read this commandment
again and again until all my idols have been vanquished.

Jesus calls us from the worship
Of the vain world's golden store:
From each idol that would keep us,
Saying Christian, love me more.

Cecil Frances Alexander

18th July

You shall not misuse the name of the Lord your
God.

Exodus 20:7

James, writing one of his letters to the early churches, commented that out of the same mouth comes praise and cursing. It seems that there is swearing at every turn from television, radio, school playgrounds, markets . . . fouls, thoughtless words of abuse. Lord, I must learn that as a Christian I need to watch my tongue for it is the wrong things I say which will be picked up, regardless of the good things I say or do. As I grow in faith and use my tongue for worship, I pray that I can be strong against evil influences around me and that I shall never misuse the name of my God.

Above all, my brothers – do not swear – not by heaven or by earth or by anything else. Let your 'Yes' be 'Yes' and your 'No' be 'No'.

James 4:12

19th July

Listen to me, you islands, hear this you distant
nations.

Isaiah 49:1

Did Isaiah have a crowd around him, I wonder? Did he proclaim God's message like a Town Crier? From historical events it seems fairly evident that the majority of people paid little attention to him . . . he suffered the frustrations common to people fired with compulsive zeal whether it be for politics, alternative medicines or religion. However, Duetero-Isaiah had the wisdom to rise above his own irritations and listen to the voice of God . . . he was ready to obey what he heard, even to sacrifice. Heavenly Father, a Sunday gives me time and opportunity to listen to Your word – give me wisdom and zeal to be able to act on Your words to me.

Master speak: and make me ready
When Thy voice is truly heard
With obedience glad and steady
Still to follow every word.
I am listening, Lord, for Thee;
Master speak, O speak to me!

Francis Ridley Havergal

20th July

Honour your father and your mother.

Exodus 20:12

'Honour' is a word which has slipped from fashion . . . sadly, in too many families respect is neither waranted nor given. We are alarmed by the way children mature to a distance so young; they listen to the opinions of everyone but mum and dad . . . blest indeed is the family which actually enjoys doing things together – scarcer those who continue to worship together as a family unit. Lord, I pray for the influence of families on each other . . . . Let your love envelope young and old as they struggle with their emotions: help us all to realise that the guidelines and attitudes set by parents today will register for a whole generation.

Listen my son to your father's instruction and do not forsake your mother's teaching.

Proverbs 1:8

21st July

All the believers were one in heart and mind. No-
one claimed that any of his possessions was his
own, but they shared everything they had.

Acts 4:32

We mustn't get carried away with the idea that the first Christians
had some perfect idyll which we have lost – they were real people
just as we are. In the next chapter on Acts comes the story about
Anaias and Sapphira, the couple who wanted to be seen to be
sharing everything whilst secretly stashing money away for themselves. An honest account of tarnished honour . . . we can sympathise to a certain extent with Ananias, perhaps his motives were
a genuine concern for his family security. O Lord, it's not easy to
share when we know others will waste . . . it's not easy to care for
everyone when I know they will annoy me and most probably
reject me . . . help me, a little at a time, to overcome feelings of
possessiveness and selfishness until I merge my heart and mind
with Your family.

Go forth and tell! The doors are open wide:
Share God's good gifts . . .
Give us, O Lord, concern of heart and mind
A love live Yours which cares for all mankind.

J. E. Seddon

22nd July

You shall not commit adultery.

Exodus 20:14

The prolific romantic novelist Barbara Cartland once said that a
man, regardless of age, colour or creed, if he had the choice,

would choose a pure woman for his wife. And what woman, if she is honest with herself, wants to feel she is 'just another'. Adultery is not only condemned on religious and moral grounds, it is a patently stupid and cruel indulgence with the risk of ruining health, family stability, children's emotions and in that situation nobody ever wins. Scars last a lifetime. Lord, I have made vows before You . . . give me strength and honesty and deepen my love for my partner as we grow together in Jesus' name.

> *Keep ye only unto him*
> *So long as ye both shall live.*
>
> from the Marriage service

23rd July

> Your path led through the sea; Your way through
> the mighty waters though Your footprints were not
> seen.
>
> *Psalm 77:19*

A speed boat causes a terrific 'wash' as it streaks through the water, then, in a few moments all is quiet with no trace of where the boat has passed. Sometimes Lord, I look for You to see obvious signs like the moving water, but I'm too late . . . I feel small and dismayed . . . hurt even. But I must learn that Your ways are not my ways and Your presence is everywhere – it's me who is looking in the wrong direction. Lord, I acknowledge that I can't see Your footprints so I just trust Your perfect, invisible way . . . hold me in my rough waters . . . I will follow where You have been in faith.

> *God moves in a mysterious way*
> *His wonders to perform;*
> *He plants His footsteps in the sea*
> *And rides upon the storm.*
>
> William Cowper

24th July

'And why do you worry about clothes?'

Matthew 6:28

Far too much emphasis is placed on what people wear – it enables us to jump to conclusions about class, wealth, attitude . . . even politics – and we're all guilty of making sweeping judgements of folk by their hairstyle and clothes. Lord, forgive me that I am concerned by the outward appearance but not all that bothered with the soul's innermost need. Why am I so shallow? Why do I worry about wearing the right clothes when really I should be far more concerned that God loves me . . . God loves those who dress well and those who dress badly . . . today I shall make the effort to look beyond clothes to the person . . . to what they are and not what they look like.

Don't show favouritism over fine or shabby clothes.

James 2: 1 – 6

25th July

You shall not covet your neighbour's house . . . or
anything that belongs to your neighbour.

Exodus 20:17

We are all being brain-washed. When we pick up a glossy magazine, watch a T.V. commercial, attend a big sporting venue or receive leaflets through the letter-box there is a multi-million pound advertising empire brain-washing us into discontent. We are a species very prone to the old emotions of jealousy and discontent . . . we want what the Jones have – or better still – we want the Joneses to want what we have got! O Lord, I am not always aware of the effect of this insidious manipulation by advertising – help me to resist temptation – open my eyes to take in all the good things I have already and squeeze out jealous thoughts by thoughts of gratitude.

Jesus said 'What good will it be for a man if he gains the whole world, yet forfeits his soul?'

Matthew 16:26

26th July

May the glory of the Lord be praised in His
dwelling-place

Ezekiel 3:12

What kind of impression do Christians give on their way to church? Some would say dull and dutiful . . . others would go as far as to say Christians going to church look joyless and solemn. This may be because of the unfortunate fact that for many the only point of contact with a church service is to attend a funeral: and it is the memory of the hushed strangeness and pervading sadness which hangs in the forefront of the thinking towards Christians. Lord, I pray for congregations today who will lift high and joyously their praise, giving You all the honour and glory . . . I will join in the worship of my Living Lord and may every gathering be seen by 'outsiders' as a vibrant congregation offering welcome, friendship and sympathy to all.

To God be the glory, great things He hath done
So loved He the world that He gave us His Son! . . .
O Come to the Father, through Jesus the Son
And give Him the glory, great things He hath done.

Frances Jane Van Alstyne

27th July

I know your deeds, that you are neither cold nor
hot . . .

Revelations 3:15

I'm feeling dreary today, Lord . . . life seems to be a catalogue of things I haven't got around to . . . I almost feel like saying 'So what!' Some days I wish I could just take-off somewhere and let other people get on with my chores – the filing, serving in the shop, having to be patient with clients who don't know what they want, having to take snide remarks from colleagues and superiors. I am burdened with guilt that I should feel like this at the start of a new week . . . Lord, help me: renew my enthusiasm and cheerfulness . . . don't let me keep my religion all neat and tidy like a garment ironed and put away in the airing cupboard . . . may my religion, my faith be my way of life and forgive me for being so wishy-washy at times.

We have not loved Thee as we ought
Nor cared that we are loved by Thee.
Thy presence we have coldly sought
And feebly longed Thy face to see.
Lord give a pure and loving heart to feel and know the love Thou art.

Thomas Benson Pollock

28th July

O Lord, You are our Father, we are the clay, You
are the potter.

Isaiah 64:8

Small potteries have sprung up all over the country in the past twenty years and they make fascinating places to visit: a skilled potter takes a shapeless lump of clay and in minutes he has transformed it into a recognisable shape. However, the finished item is several processes away . . . drying, firing, glazing, firing until the finished egg-cup or jug emerges fit for sale and use. Lord, You are not only my Father but also my Creator, the Divine Potter who can take my messy old life and convert it into something worthwhile . . . give me humility to undergo all the necessary processes before I can be used for Your glory . . . humility, perseverance and adaptability.

> *Mould as Thou wilt the passive clay . . .*
> *Let all my works in Thee be wrought*
> *By Thee to full perfection brought.*

Charles Wesley

29th July

Jesus said: 'He who has ears to hear, let him hear.'

Mark 4:9

Again, Jesus appears to be saying the obvious – yet how keenly He shows His understanding of our human minds, and sometimes it is the obvious that has to be pushed right under our noses before we take any notice at all. Often I don't listen to what people say . . . if I'm going to be honest, Lord, it's because I'm not interested . . . on the other hand, I expect You to be interested in me and to listen when I pour out my prayers. Today I ask for a discerning and sympathetic ear – teach me how to listen to others in the same kind attitude I need given to me.

Just as love to God begins with listening to His word, so the beginning of love for the brethren is learning to listen to them . . .

Many people are looking for an ear that will listen. He who can no longer listen to his brother will soon be no longer listening to God either. We should listen with the ears of God that we may speak the word of God.

Dietrich Bonhoeffer

30th July

How great is the love the Father has lavished on
us . . .

1 John 3:1

The missionary Helen Roseveare recounts the story of how she took one of the workers by Land Rover to collect his desperately sick child, and drove father and child to hospital. The man had never even sat in a vehicle before let alone entered a hospital but when they arrived there Helen Roseveare told him not to return to work until the child was better. The child responded to the treatment and the father was able to be back at work after only four days but being so poor, the four days with the hospital had lost him 4 days wages and he and his wife had gone into debt. At the end of the month, Helen had forgotten the days off and the man collected his normal wage. He couldn't believe it – he ran all the way home where he and his wife knelt in the dust to give their hearts to Jesus Christ. Suddenly they saw a glimpse of God's redeeming love.

Love so amazing, so divine
Demands my soul, my life, my all.

Isaac Watts

31st July

'And when you pray, do not keep on babbling like
pagans, for they think they will be heard because of
their many words . . . '

Matthew 6:7

Am I guilty of being long-winded, repetitive . . . even muddle-minded in my prayers? Forgive me if I've tried to impress with a 'long' prayer . . . today, I'll just slip in the odd word here and there to thank You for routine details of my life, daily blessings that seem too small to mention, for amenities and comforts that never feature in prayers. Lord, show me that nothing is too small to bring to You, there is nothing that I should take for granted . . . so thank You for the pleasant smell of the furniture polish, the means of cooking and heating the water, for the cheery smile from the postman and the girl in the newsagents. So many trifling things during the day which all add up to make it more interesting, give me a sense of security and belonging in the neighbourhood.

Everything must reveal God to us. Long prayers are not needed in order to smile at Christ in the smallest details of daily life.

Michel Quoist

1st August

Then the angel showed me the river of the water of
life . . . flowing from the throne of God and of the
Lamb . . .

Revelation 22:1

During this month much church life 'goes on holiday' – all the usual weekday groups round off in July to begin again in September. What a good thing God does not go on holiday! He is with us whatever the date, whatever we are doing, wherever we are, at home or on holiday. Holidays can be quite good for us in that we get away to see how others work, play, eat and worship. It reduces our importance within the framework of world-wide Christianity . . . we feel more aware of the rest of the world, and come home refreshed to get on with ordinary living. Apart from wanting to come home relaxed and with a good tan, I pray Lord for a vision of the refreshing water of life . . . a renewal for my soul, I want to stretch out my hands for this life-giving stream . . . I know You will not fail me.

> *See the streams of living water*
> *Springing from eternal love . . .*
> *Grace, which like the Lord, the Giver,*
> *Never fails from age to age.*

John Newton

2nd August

Elijah told his servant, 'Go and look towards the
sea.'

1 Kings 18:43

The sea . . . always changing, fascinating, untamed, unpredictable; all round our coasts today people will be gazing at the sea. I'm reminded how Jesus taught by the sea of Galilee . . . he walked on the sea, . . . went out in a boat on the sea, – Lord, as I look towards the horizon I feel very small indeed. The sea has no terminal, no edges, it doesn't dry up . . . its waves touch every continent and island in one way dividing nations but in another, a mysterious force of unity. The power and constancy of the sea is

God-ordained and by the shore, with the tang of the sea in my nostrils, somehow it seems only natural to praise the Lord of Heaven and Earth and Sea. Lord, I feel one with Your world.

In the sea's horizon you get a terrific sense of infinity and eternity and I have learned from watching it that there is no such thing as time or space or solid matter as they are all dissolved by light.

Thelma Beswick
artist and cancer sufferer

3rd August

For the eyes of the Lord are on the righteous and
His ears are attentive to their prayer.

1 Peter 3:13

Lord, forgive me that my prayers are loaded with self, but it does help me to unburden myself, to unwind, get things off my chest. I don't pretend to understand how or why You should listen to me – I am just content to accept what Jesus said, that with God all things are possible. I believe You hear the sincere and humble cry from every heart . . . help me to pray more easily . . . let it become part of my mind keeping close to You through the rigours of each day . . . Heavenly Father, my prayer is all I have to bring You.

Prayer is also learning, and practising, to replace a lonely sense of separation, of struggling on our own, being afraid, inadequate and doubtful, with the home-coming sense of belonging as the beloved child of God, who is all good.

Joyce Grenfell

4th August

Jesus replied: 'A certain man was preparing a great
banquet and invited many guests. He sent His
servant to tell those who had been invited 'Come,
for everything is now ready' . . . But they all alike
began to make excuses.

Luke 14:16

Listening to a talk on the radio I heard the thought expressed that
sin is not only something we 'do' but sin can also be something
which we fail to 'do'. Failure can be sin. Jesus knows how we
wriggle . . . He offers us eternal life . . . life more abundantly . . .
His peace . . . but in the welter of our excuses lies our rejection of
the Heavenly Banquet. Excuses, whether they be to our friends or
to God, mean 'No . . . *I* don't want to!' Lord, how can I be so
blind? How can I reject Your invitation? When excuses spring to
my tongue, help me to say 'Yes', to come with excitement, expectation and commitment.

Come, sinners to the gospel feast
Let every soul be Jesu's guest;
Yield to His love's resistless power
And fight against your God no more.

Charles Wesley

5th August

'Everyone who hears these words of mine and does
not put them into practice is like a foolish man who
built his house on sand.'

Matthew 7:26

Everyone who heard Jesus talking about a man building his house on the sand knew that was a stupid thing to do . . . just as we realise the stupidity of drinking and driving, of smoking in bed . . . common sense rules, which when broken lead to trouble. We are all experts at watching our neighbours behave irresponsibly . . . but what about me Lord? I've heard Your word times without number – and I've ignored it. Did I think You were meaning some-one else? Forgive my complacency, my arrogance . . . I am listening now – I am listening and praying that I will learn by my mistakes – I don't want a faith built on sand, but on the Rock of my Salvation.

> *Christ be my teacher in age as in youth,*
> *Drifting or doubting, for He is the truth:*
> *Grant me to trust Him, though shifting as sand,*
> *Doubt cannot daunt me, in Jesus I stand.*
>
> Timothy Dudley-Smith

6th August

> On the walls all around the temple, in both inner
> and outer rooms, he carved cherubim, palm trees
> and open flowers.
>
> *1 King 6:29*

So even the earliest temple was adorned with carvings of beautiful flowers; and down through all the centuries, where people have met to worship, flowers have been a favourite decoration. This is a favourite time of year for Flower Festivals . . . churches festooned in colour, gorgeous interpretations by men and women in an act of praise. Thank You, Lord, for the scent and individual delicacy of flowers, thank You for the ideas which come forward for Flower Festivals and the fellowship enjoyed by those who work together to beautify Your earthly temples today.

I pray for all those who will meander around a church to see the arrangements but have no interest in their creator – I pray for the sick and infirm who will receive flowers as a token of love and remembrance from their friends –

Lord, I pray for the power of Love demonstrated by Your flowers.

> *I sat upon my little porch*
> *And whiled the sunny hours . . .*
> *A friend came by and stopped to let me*
> *Smell his bunch of flowers.*

Yamaguchi
Japanese Christian leper

7th August

. . . if we love each other, God lives in us, and His
love is made complete in us.

1 John 4:12

Today, I am thinking about the joys of human love – thank You, Lord, for my husband . . . for all we have shared, the laughs we've had, and surmounting all the difficulties, the gentle pleasure of being in each other's company. Help me, Lord, not to neglect making my feelings plain – too many couples end up with regrets over things they never got around to saying . . . human love is a treasure, precious and rewarding every day . . . may our lives be blessed in the recognition of Your spirit holding us together in completeness.

> *Happy the home where man and wife together*
> *Are of one mind, believing in Your love;*
> *Through love and pain, prosperity and hardship,*
> *Through good and evil days Your care we prove.*

Karl Spitta

8th August

The God of Israel spoke: ' . . . when he rules in the
fear of God he is like the light of morning at sunrise.'

2 Samuel 23:4

I don't know how people can spend so much of their time in bed
behind closed curtains, losing half their existence in torpor. Each
sunrise is unique, the formation of the clouds, the tints and streaks
of colour in the dawn sky, merging and changing as you watch
into the brilliance of morning. Lord, what a fabulous world this
is! Teach me to regard each dawn as a holy beginning for my little
hum-drum being . . . give my heart and mind a freshness, a small
reflection of Your warmth and light.

> *Summer suns are glowing over land and sea,*
> *Happy light is flowing, bountiful and free;*
> *Everything rejoices in the mellow rays*
> *All earth's thousand voices*
> *Swell the psalm of praise.*

William Walsham How

9th August

The Lord watches over the alien and sustains the
fatherless and the widow.

Psalm 146:9

These three categories are amongst the most vulnerable in society.
The Law of Moses was highly moral and many aspects were truly
kind-hearted and everybody was expected to carry out responsibility towards the less fortunate in the community as part of
their worship. The ultimate comfort being that God cares for
them especially. Lord, I pray for widows, I name before You those

I know personally; I pray for children growing up without the guidance of a father, the illegitimate, the orphans, those in care; I pray for the refugees, the aliens, the uprooted and persecuted and disadvantaged. Help me to make their burdens my concern, for Jesus Christ's sake.

> *The holier worship which He deigns to bless*
> *Restores the lost, and binds the spirit broken*
> *And feeds the widow and the fatherless.*
>
> John Greenleaf Whittier

10th August

Jesus told him (expert on the Law) 'Go and do likewise.'

Luke 10:37

The parable Jesus told of the Good Samaritan must be one of the favourites of all time. Everybody knows how the two 'religious' men passed by on the other side when their help was so badly needed . . . we all remember that the hero of the story was the despised foreigner who went out of his way, and out of pocket too, to give a hand to a stricken stranger. A captivating, moving story – but how did Jesus finish? Lord, I like the story – forgive me that I have treated it like a story and I haven't done anything worthwhile to help any body . . . I have conveniently forgotten the commission to behave like the Samaritan. Give me compassion to go and *do*.

> *And Peter twirled the jangling keys in weariness and wrath,*
> *'Ye have read, ye have heard, ye have thought,' he said and the tale*
> *is yet to run:*
> *'By the worth of the body that once ye had, give answer –*
> *What ha' ye done?'*
>
> Rudyard Kipling
> 'Tomlinson'

11th August

When tempted no-one should say 'God is tempting
me.'

James 1:13

When something goes wrong, the immediate reaction today seems
to be 'It's not my fault.' But, then, not only today, that kind of
response goes right back to Adam . . . 'please God, it wasn't my
fault, it was your fault for giving me the woman!!' Lord, why do
we lack the guts to carry the can ourselves . . . forgive me my
swiftness to blame others, the nearest most handy person . . . even
You; give me Your strength that today I may have the humility to
say, 'I'm sorry, it was my fault.'

Lead us not into temptation,
But deliver us from evil.

12th August

Moses' anger burned hot and he threw the tablets
out of his hand . . .

Exodus 32:19

Oh yes, I can sympathise with Moses – I know what burning
anger is like. But why oh why is it that in anger we destroy what
we most care about. Those precious, God-given tablets chucked
on the ground in temper . . . But if God was able to use hot-
tempered Moses, then there's hope for me. Paul wrote to the
Galatians that self-control was a gift of the Spirit . . . how much
we need that gift today. After all, where would we be, Lord if we
resorted to such childish behaviour as hurling words, throwing
saucepans . . . fists . . . bullets, missiles . . . bombs: I pray for the
gift of self-control.

Breathe through the heats of our desire Thy coolness and Thy
balm,
Let sense be dumb, let flesh retire,
Speak through the earthquake, wind and fire,
O still small voice of calm.

John Greenleaf Whittier

13th August

Little children were brought to Jesus for Him to
place His hands on them.

Matthew 19:13

Many thousands of parents have to face the agonising reality that
their little child is not like others – their future only offers heartache. The late President de Gaulle had a daughter with a common
mental handicap and when she died the famous man stood by her
grave and whispered, 'now she is like all the rest'. Indeed, for some
children it is only in death that they can be born to true life and
freedom from pain and suffering. Lord, I believe that each life has
a purpose within Your plan . . . each life belongs to You . . . I
pray for 'special' children with extra special need for love.

Thus may all children brought to You
Be nurtured in Your way:
And so, in goodness and in truth
Your spirit's fruits display.

Derek R. Farrow

14th August

Jesus said: 'A new commandment I give you, Love
one another.'

John 13:34

A man who listened to John Wesley preaching in the open air wrote: 'the Bible looked new and I felt a great love to all mankind'. Lord, if only I could see people through the eyes of Your love – when I get impatient and irritated by people help me to remember Your commandment. . . . I ask for a new attitude to the people who make up my day . . . may that attitude exclude my personal whims and be the all-embracing compassion of Jesus, my pattern, my priest and my King.

> *Let there be love shared among us*
> *Let there be love in your eyes,*
> *May now Your love sweep this nation*
> *Cause us, O Lord, to arise –*
> *Give us a fresh understanding of brotherly love that is real*
> *Let there be love shared among us,*
> *Let there be love.*

D. Bilbrough

15th August

> Finally, be strong in the Lord and in His mighty power . . . for our struggle is not against flesh and blood, but against rulers, against the authorities, against the powers of this dark world . . . the spiritual forces of evil . . .
>
> *Ephesians 6:10/12*

There are times, Lord, when I do feel up against the forces of evil, forces which seem to be gaining control. How do I stop my children from enjoying the appalling violence on television without creating moods of reproach and antagonism in the family? What can I do about blasphemy, foul language, general irreverence for life itself where child abuse is multiplying. You are my only hope, Lord, my only strength . . . help me to stand firm to Your word and not be swayed into compromise. Let no-one underestimate the power of evil.

Soldiers of Christ arise and put your armour on;
Strong in the strength which God supplies
Through His eternal Son.
Strong in the Lord of Hosts, and in His mighty power
Who, in the strength of Jesus trusts is more than conqueror.

Charles Wesley

16th August

How great are your works O Lord, how profound
your thoughts.

Psalm 92:5

This psalm is entitled 'A song for the Sabbath day'. It's a psalm which tells of God's faithfulness and sovereign power even though the wicked flourish now, God is in control and will be exalted for ever. This was the favourite psalm of a mother who spent the last months of her life with the Macmillan nursing service, tending the terminally ill in their own homes. She nursed the nice and the nasty and came to realise that at the point of death we are all the same in God's eyes. Her faith was an unforgettable example in that . . . she was not downcast because she believed in a great God who was in control no matter what happened to her. Lord, thank you for those today in the Macmillan Nursing service and all similar groups; we are so frail and You are so great.

O God of love, O God of Calvary,
How great Thou art! How great Thou art!
In all the world there is no one like Thee,
How great Thou art! How great Thou art!

N. J. Clayton

17th August

'Do not judge, or you too will be judged. For in the
same way you judge others, you will be judged, and
the measure you use, it will be measured to you.'

Matthew 7:1/2

During the First World War, men not in uniform were frowned upon and the story is told of how two young women gave white feathers to two young men they saw sitting at a cafe table. They meant to publicly shame the young men for their cowardice and felt self-righteous in doing so. They did not see the crutches beneath the table, nor the empty trouser leg . . . forgive me, Lord when I make snap judgements – I jump in with both feet to condemn regardless of the strife it may cause; give me grace to accept people as they are, as I too, look for acceptance.

O! Master grant that I may never seek so much to be consoled as to console; to be understood as to understand, to be loved, as to love with all my soul . . . make me a channel of Your peace, it is in pardoning that we are pardoned; in giving to all men that we receive and in dying that we're born to eternal life.

Prayer of St Francis adapted by
Sebastian Temple

18th August

Hear my cry, O God: listen to my prayer.

Psalm 61:1

One August morning I stood in Westminster Abbey as the hands of the clock approached the noon hour. The bustle of tourists stopped as a short time of prayer was observed. There we stood . . . Japanese, Germans, Brownies, Nuns, people of every race, colour, size and age . . . quietly, reverently praying. A moment of unexpected unity enfolding total strangers in an unforgettable experience. Lord, I know You listened that day, in that Holy place . . . please hear me again today.

Love to pray – feel often during the day the need for prayer, and take trouble to pray. Prayer enlarges the heart until it is capable of containing God's gift of Himself.

Mother Teresa

19th August

He was despised and rejected by men, a man of
sorrows and familiar with suffering.

Isaiah 53:3

It's stupid of us to imagine that no one understands quite how we feel . . . sorrow and suffering is not something we alone feel, and the miracle of the Son of God who suffered emotional and physical hell, gives us a measure of comfort in our trials. During this week, well over 100 people will die on the roads of the British Isles alone, they will add to the statistics – multiply those figures with those who have been involved in road accidents and survived, but whose lives have been shattered and we have a horrific statistic of suffering and grief. Lord, You know how people are feeling today, help us to pour out all our troubles and know Your comforting peace.

Jesus knows your sorrow, knows your every care,
Knows your deep contrition, hears your feeblest prayer,
Do not fear to trust Him
Tell Him all your grief,
Cast on Him your burden,
He will bring relief.

W. O. Cushing

20th August

The days are coming, declares the Sovereign Lord,
when I will send a famine through the land, not a
famine of food, but a famine of hearing the words
of the Lord.

Amos 8:11

The Bible is a best seller whilst also being the worst-neglected Word of God. I ask myself about my Bible – is it a natural part of the day or is it tucked away, nice and clean, undiscovered and forgotten? I am put to shame by the real longing of those persecuted Christians who have no Bible . . . how they treasure a single page, and can recite chapters off by heart. Lord, I know that I don't live as though the word of Life belonged to me, bring me to love Your word . . . bring me through its sacred pages closer to Jesus.

It is a fact that churches of 200–300 or more members do not possess one single Bible. The joy the Bibles gave was great. A brother got up, took the Bible in his hand and kissed it. One cannot forget such things . . .

from a letter by a western visitor to an
unregistered Baptist congregation
in Russia with
12 Bibles

21st August

Be shepherds of God's flock under your care,
serving . . . not because you must, but because you
are willing.

1 Peter 5:2

Sadly there are people in positions of influence within church structures who hold office unwillingly. What ought to be a service of love becomes a chore and not surprisingly the resultant atmosphere becomes barren. Lord, forgive the selfishness of the people who will push anyone into office rather than take responsibility themselves . . . forgive me when I resent time and effort in service. Open my selfish mind to the needs of service within the community, the lost souls, the bewildered and wandering souls of every age who need willing disciples to show them the Saviour's pity.

Jesus, Thy wandering sheep behold,
See Lord, with tenderest pity, see
The sheep that cannot find the fold
Till sought and gathered in by Thee.

Charles Wesley

22nd August

When he (the cripple) saw Peter and John about to
enter the temple, he asked them for money.

Acts 3:3

In ancient times, and in poor countries today, begging is the only way some unfortunates can survive. Peter and John had no money to give, but instead they gave the knowledge of the risen Jesus and if only mankind would take Jesus into their hearts and lives, the begging today would not be necessary. Some charities, and they are all good causes, have almost made begging into big business, whereas, if people followed the commands of Jesus there would be no charities caring for victims of violence and war, old folk with no families nor help, children rescued from their own parents, millions starving . . . Lord, I am truly blessed with health, home, happiness and material comforts . . . how would I react to the collecting tins if You were physically standing with me as I opened my purse?

Take my silver and my gold
Not a mite would I withhold
Take my intellect and use
Every power as Thou shalt choose.

Francis Ridley Havergal

23rd August

For this reason I kneel before the Father from
whom the whole family in heaven and on earth
derives its name.

Ephesians 3:14

The Christian need never feel alone because to follow Jesus is to be
joined in a world-wide family . . . the Family of God on earth and
in Heaven. Today, Lord, I look to You as my loving Heavenly
Father, and thank You for this far-flung family to which I belong;
thank You also for the family of my blood and the family of
believers who are my friends. With so much heartache and recri-
mination around with broken families, I come with fresh eyes,
grateful for the laughter and stability which supports me. I pray
for a special blessing on families . . . draw us closer together in
love and tolerance.

Dear Heavenly Father, as we meet to adore You
Let us catch a fresh vision of the things we should do;
Draw us closer together, warm our hearts to each other,
We are joined in one family,
Help us live in Your love.

Elizabeth Rundle

24th August

Let us not become weary in doing good.

Galatians 6:9

It's nearly two hundred and sixty years since John and Charles
Wesley began prison visiting and caring for the sick and under-
privileged but it is quite alarming how basic goodness is still so
badly needed in this, our sophisticated age. We don't mind the
odd acts of kindness but it's the continuity of putting ourselves

out that sticks in the gullet . . . we become weary of doing good. Lord, it's so hard to persevere . . . help me to remember that this very day, there are neighbours who need help . . . a lift some-where . . . some cooking done . . . opportunities for doing good are endless.

On 24th August 1730, my brother and I walked to the castle (Oxford Jail) . . . we agreed to go together once or twice a week; which we had not done long before Mr Morgan desired me to go with him to see a poor woman in the town who was sick. May we not try to do good to those that are hungry, naked or sick? In particular, whether, if we know any necessitous family, we may give them a little food, clothes or physic as they want.

John Wesley

25th August

How sweet are Your promises to my taste; sweeter
than honey to my mouth!

Psalm 119:103

Honey is so pure it was once used as a dressing on open wounds – so it was amazingly apt for the psalmist to liken God's pure word to something as clean, pure and natural as honey. Jesus was the word made flesh, the fulfilment of the promises of God, and it is to that pure and risen Jesus, the living Lord of my life that R. F. Miller wrote the gospel song: 'I'd rather have Jesus than anything this world affords today'. Lord, I whisper that as my prayer today.

*He's fairer than lilies of rarest bloom,
He's sweeter than honey from out the comb;
He's all that my hungering spirit needs,
I'd rather have Jesus and let Him lead.*

Rhea F. Miller

26th August

The third time Jesus said to him 'Simon, son of
John, do you love me?'

John 21:16

Peter was hurt that Jesus asked him three times and he replied,
'Lord, you know everything – You know that I love You.' I could
put it another way and say, 'Lord, You know everything, You
know that I try to love You . . . You know how often I've been a
miserable failure . . . You know when I haven't tried at all . . . '
When people let me down, I get hurt and can't see any reason for
their behaviour . . . Lord, I have no excuses for my behaviour but
I pray that I may learn to love You more and more each day.

> *I love Thee because Thou hast first loved me,*
> *And purchased my pardon on Calvary's tree;*
> *I love Thee for wearing the thorns on Thy brow;*
> *If ever I loved Thee, if ever I loved Thee,*
> *If ever I loved Thee, my Jesus 'tis now.*

Anon

27th August

Jesus said, 'And if you greet only your brothers,
what are you doing more than others? Do not even
pagans do that?'

Matthew 5:47

What marvellously kind, generous and well-intentioned folk
there are today who will gladly offer all the assistance they can if a
personal or even national disaster occurs. Yet they would not call
themselves Christians . . . Jesus knows we live surrounded by
those who are not followers of His and He also knows that though
this is a sinful world, most people are respectable and kind . . . so
He asks us to go beyond that . . . He asks us to live our commitment so that the difference between Christians and non-
Christians is obvious. Lord, infuse my life with that extra dimen-
sion of Your loving Holy Spirit.

What have you done today that nobody but a Christian would do?

Women's World Day of Prayer leaflet

28th August

'Keep watch.'

Matthew 25:13

Comedians have a better chance of becoming a household name if they adopt a catch-phrase: 'Hallo Playmates' . . . 'I'm free' . . . 'Shut that door!' . . . 'Nice to see you – to see you, nice'. Jesus must have been a gifted storyteller and a man whose words were easily memorised by his listeners. We can even pick out a catch-phrase too, 'keep watch' . . . 'watch and pray'; warnings against complacency about the power of evil in daily things, warning to draw close to God before events overtake us, entreaties to really hear the message of Good News. Lord, I will try to be alert – to be watchful of myself and watchful for Your kingdom.

Hear, above all, hear Thy Lord,
Him thou lovest to obey,
Hide within thy heart His word,
Watch and Pray.

Charlotte Elliott

29th August

Better to live on a corner of the roof than share a
house with a quarrelsome wife.

Proverbs 21:9

This sentence from Proverbs arouses a rainbow of reactions from the 'yellowish' smile at the picture it conjures up to 'purple' indignation that only a man would have written a sentence like that! Somewhere in the middle lies the truth . . . a woman holds the major responsibility for a happy and contented, smooth-running household. And we all know women whose tongues are so waspish that they are never happier than in a quarrel with someone. . . . Lord, when I feel shrewish and wound-up inside, melt my heart with kindness, gentle humour and patience.

Don't have anything to do with foolish and stupid arguments, because you know they produce quarrels. And the Lord's servant must not quarrel: instead he must be kind to everyone . . .
2 Timothy 2:22

30th August

The promise is for you and your children and for all
who are far off . . . for all whom the Lord our God
will call . . .
Acts 2:39

On a summer evening, in a quiet little Scottish manse, the minister Dr Matheson was aching with sorrow because of a very sad bereavement – at his lowest moment he felt the words of a hymn rushing into his mind and in a short while he had written the words 'O Love that wilt not let me go'. He freely admitted that the hymn was the fruit of pain, yet God had used his emotion to glimpse the miracle that behind all our present troubles, His promises stand for us still. Lord, I claim Your promises . . . I will not, I cannot close my heart to You.

O Joy that seekest me through pain
I cannot close my heart to Thee
I trace the rainbow through the rain
And feel the promise is not vain,
*   That morn shall tearless be.*

Dr George Matheson

31st August

'I am the door – if anyone enters by Me he will be
saved.'

John 10:8

All religions strive towards making a person better able to cope
with their life and also point to a better world if the people would
accept a model code of conduct. There is, however, a growing
tendency to believe that being a Christian is somehow not the only
way to eternal life – Jesus stated that He was the door, the only
Way, the Truth and the Life and no-one could approach God but
through His saving grace. Lord, deliver me from woolly thinking . . . direct my whole being towards Jesus, not for what I can
selfishly gain, but to be saved from this world and in His love
bring others to that same Door.

*It is God's own will that everyone of His dear children should find
that the door to repentance is always open.*

Clement
1st century A.D.

1st September

After three days they found Him in the Temple
courts sitting among the teachers, listening to them
and asking questions.

Luke 2:46

Soon children will be returning to school after the summer holidays. Some will be facing the prospect of school for the very first
time, and as with anything that is new, it will bring flutters of
fright to mother and child. School – where a child is no longer the
focus of the family's attention but becomes a member of a class, a
group, and love it or hate it, it will shape their future, bring them
friends, skills and interests. Bless these young lives, Lord, bless
them, their families and the teachers who will influence them.

While they ply the scholars task
Jesus Christ, be near, I ask
Help the memory, clear the brain,
Knowledge still to seek and gain.

Handley C.G. Moule

2nd September

The Lord is my shepherd, I will lack nothing. . . .

Psalm 23:1

The words of this psalm, sung to the tune Crimond, are amongst
the best known in the Bible . . . beautiful words of comfort for
'down' periods. September brings the end of several things . . . the
end of summer, the long evenings, the end of holidays, the end of
youngsters' first years at home . . . endings are sad – bear with
me, Lord, if I feel dejected, teach me that an end to one thing
automatically means the beginning of something else. So, there'll
be no tears for what has to close, rather thanks for memories. . . . I
shall not feel lonely for my shepherd is with me and He will take
care of everything.

The king of love my shepherd is
Whose goodness faileth never
I nothing lack if I am His
And He is mine for ever.

Henry W. Baker

3rd September

We have confidence in the Lord.

2 Thessalonians 3:4

Advertisements leer out of newspapers and magazines offering
courses to build up our confidence – hypnotists rake in a fair old
profit from the proceeds of the insecure clients who flock to find
self-confidence . . . there are so many people who feel hesitant

and unsure of themselves and of others. What a glorious thing to feel confident – totally confident in the partner we love, confident in the unseen Presence which at all times guides loves and strengthens us. Yes, Lord, today I feel strong and confident in You.

Jesus, my strength, my hope
On Thee I cast my care;
With humble confidence look up
And know Thou hear'st my prayer.

Charles Wesley

4th September

'By their fruit you will recognise them.'

Matthew 7:16

Heavenly Father, I need to ask myself if anyone would recognise me by my 'fruit' . . . can the compassion of Jesus be glimpsed through my dealings with people day by day? I'm afraid some of my fruit is unripe, some withered, only a few are worth calling 'fruit'. Lord, help me not to be like the Pharisees, holy outside and hollow inside, I long to be fair and even-tempered . . . Lord of all Goodness and Love, use my life to spread the fruits of Your spirit that believers will be seen as Your representatives.

We are one in the spirit, we are one in the Lord,
And we pray that all unity one day be restored;
And they'll know we are Christians by our love.

Peter Scholts

5th September

'. . . a certain rich man produced a good crop. He
thought to himself, "What shall I do? I have no
place to store my crops".'

Luke 12:16

The calamity of the parable Jesus told about the rich man is the continuing truth that many possessions bring worries about how to keep them safe. Bigger and better barns . . . more and more storage acres to hoard grain, milk, butter, potatoes . . . stronger and more complicated locks, involved security systems all conspiring to retain our possessions at any cost. Does this bring happiness? Lord, whatever I have comes from You anyway – teach me that by sharing I will not be losing but increasing my joy, doubling Your blessing . . . the only thing I would pray to lose would be my possessiveness for things that will not last.

Father providing food for Your children,
Your wisdom guiding, teaches us to share with one another,
So that rejoicing, with us our brother
May know Your care.

Albert F. Bayly

6th September

I urge, then, that requests, prayers, intercessions
and thanksgiving be made for everyone – for kings
and all those in authority.

1 Timothy 2:1

We have developed a national sport of knocking the Government and from our comfortable chairs or kitchen table, it's so easy to criticise authority, whether it be police, bank managers, judges or local councillors. I had never thought it was my Christian duty to prayerfully support those in authority . . . Lord, show me how much could be achieved in situations if the barriers of 'Them' and 'Us' could be broken down by the spirit of prayer – by the genuine quest for Your will, and show me too that those in authority carry enormous burdens of responsibility far beyond that which I could tolerate – every group or collection of people has to have leaders but no group is helped by constant criticism and mistrust . . . prayers for everyone are important indeed.

For this reason, ever since I heard about your faith in the Lord Jesus and your love for all the saints, I have not stopped giving thanks for you, remembering you in prayers. I keep asking that the God of our Lord Jesus Christ may give you the Spirit of wisdom and revelation.

Paul in his letter to the Ephesians, Chapter 1:15, 16

7th September

Jesus said: 'Because I live, you also will live.'

John 14:19

In the promises Jesus made to His disciples, He was openly aligning Himself with the living God and belief in these promises have changed lives completely. Joan was used to indifference, even verbal abuse when she distributed religious tracts in the Exeter pubs, but she did not expect to be spat on as one man did, but her unswerving belief in Christ's promises strengthened her to carry on unbowed. There is no reason for us to be afraid or worried . . . Jesus has promised to be with us in this life and in the life to come . . . Lord, help me to live this day trusting Your promises for today and for eternity.

> *Because He lives, I can face tomorrow,*
> *Because He lives, all fear is gone*
> *Because I know He holds the future,*
> *And life is worth the living just because He lives.*

William Gaither

8th September

Jesus answered him (the criminal) 'I tell you the truth, today you will be with me in paradise.'

Luke 23:43

Sometimes events in our lives take us completely by surprise – one moment a thrilling gymkhana, the next a young rider rushed off to hospital with a broken arm – one moment a bustling shop, the next the horror of a robbery. None of us are immune from accidents, illness, muggings, burglaries and these few desperate seconds affect us for the rest of our lives. In the moment of his greatest agony, the criminal was reassured by Jesus that in that very day they would be together in paradise – no waiting . . . likewise Lord, I seek that same assurance that in the midst of my upheavals, You will be there . . . no waiting.

> *New arts shall bloom of loftier mould*
> *And mightier music thrill the skies;*
> *And every life shall be a song,*
> *When all the earth is paradise.*

John Symonds

9th September

What I mean brothers is that the time is short.
1 Corinthians 7:29

Funny how we never really treasure time until it is running out – Jesus told the story of the five organised virgins and the five who were caught unawares by the bridegroom's arrival; Paul felt that Jesus would return to the world comparatively quickly, so the believers in Corinth didn't have long to prepare, hence the teaching of wise use of time. Lord, I wish I could organise my time better, already the summer has gone . . . I'm not ready for autumn, I'm not ready for the shortness of my life compared with all the things I hope to do. I have wasted so much time, Lord . . . give me wisdom to treat each day as a gift, not to watch the clock but to be thankful for each hour.

At railway stations parents gaze after sons and daughters leaving for college and wonder where the years have gone . . . keep an eye on time . . . time is passing by.

John Pearce

10th September

They began to grumble against the landowner:
'these men who were hired last worked only one
hour and you have made them equal to us who
have borne the burden of the work . . .'

Matthew 20:12

This parable at first sight seems remarkably unfair – the men who
had worked longest seem to have a just complaint against those
who rolled up for the last hour. We know how they felt because
we know how galling it is to slog away on some project then
somebody comes along at the last minute and walks off with all
the glory . . . often I look at people and the words 'why should
they?' are on the tip of my tongue. Lord, I know it's wrong to feel
this way, it is hurt pride . . . open my heart to embrace all helpers
in Your name, however much or little they do because, although I
may not like it, I have to accept that Your love and reward is
equally for them as for me.

Dismiss me not Thy service, Lord,
But train me for Thy will;
For even I, in fields so broad, some duties may fulfil;
And I will ask for no reward
Except to serve Thee still.

Thomas T. Lynch

11th September

. . . but no man can tame the tongue.

James 3:8

What a lot of harm is caused by our tongues – idle chatter,
malicious gossip, cruel rebuffs, shouts of anger . . . we are the
same kind of people making the same kind of trouble for ourselves
as the folk of the early church. Mankind never learns . . . our
tongues literally run away with us against all our better judge-

ment, and agonising hours are spent in futile regret – the harm has been done. Lord, make me especially aware of the impact of what I say . . . forgive me for being careless and thoughtless about the feelings of others . . . today, if I can't say anything pleasant about a person, give me sense to be silent.

> *God be in my head and in my understanding;*
> *God be in mine eyes and in my looking;*
> *God be in my mouth and in my speaking.*
> *God be in my heart and in my thinking,*
> *God be at mine end and at my departing.*

from a Sarum Primer 1558

12th September

May the words of my mouth and the meditation of my heart be pleasing in Your sight O Lord, my Rock and my Redeemer.

Psalm 19:14

Once I have learnt the discipline of a controlled tongue, help me Lord to put my words to good use. There is so much goodness, beauty and encouragement to meditate on; so many kindnesses by neighbours, lives of dedication in special schools for the blind, deaf or physically disabled . . . may I speak of the good things I witness so that the spirit of encouragement may grow and blossom . . . may I meditate on the blessings I have received and may my heart be full of joy as my faith grows ever deeper, grounded on Jesus, my Rock and my Redeemer.

> *O Jesus, blest Redeemer, sent from the heart of God,*
> *Hold us, who wait before Thee, near to the heart of God.*

C. B. McAfee

13th September

*. . . at the proper time we will reap a harvest if we
do not give up.*

Galatians 6:9

Take the H out of the word Harvest and you have the word
Starve. We come into the season of Harvest Festivals with much
relief and thanksgiving for another year of plenty . . . in the
knowledge too that as we swell a harvest song of praise, there are
those today who will die through the effects of malnutrition,
disease, ignorance and superstition. I feel so helpless, Lord, so
frustrated that after all the staggering efforts to aid famine
regions, men, women, children and cattle are still dying. As my
table sags with so much tasty nourishment, I remember the words
of Paul that we must not give up . . . persevere, and one day the
whole world will be fed.

> *Some have plenty, some have nothing,*
> *Bodies weak and soon to die;*
> *I see little children starving,*
> *Lord, it makes me want to cry.*

Elizabeth Rundle

14th September

Your will be done . . .

Matthew 6:10

The Lord's Prayer is repeated so often – it can become a recitation
by mouth while our minds are on something totally different. I
pray, Lord, that these familiar words may be etched in my heart
because I feel them as well as say them. I need Your help to
relinquish selfish wants . . . I need to learn how to take a back seat
and accept Your will before my own, to realise that sometimes it is
only when we stand aside that You can work through us to
complete Your will. Here in the mellowness of this September
day, I repeat the great prayer . . . Your will be done –

On the morning of September 14th, 1943 I came to the point of abject acceptance. 'I'm tired of asking . . . I'm beaten, finished God. You decide what You want for me.' Tears flowed. And the result? It was if I had touched a button that opened windows in heaven . . . I experienced the living Christ in a way that wiped away all doubt and revolutionised my life.'

Catherine Marshall

15th September

So God created . . . every kind of winged bird
according to its kind.

Genesis 1:21

A sure and sad sign that the summer is over is the sight of swallows lined up along the telephone wires preparing for their flight to a warmer winter. Tiny birds, programmed with computer accuracy to enable them to fly hundreds, sometimes thousands of miles. I marvel at the instinct . . . I marvel at the perfection of their feathers and individual song. When I think about how my God creates I bow my head at man's propensity to destroy. O Lord, You who gave the birds their brain and intelligence according to their need, I pray that I may use my brain to enjoy all your creatures and praise You, the creator of all.

> *How wonderful this world of Thine*
> *Where all things serve Thy great design*
> *The migrant bird, in winter fled,*
> *Shall come again with spring*
> *And build in this same shady tree.*

Fred Pratt Green

16th September

Now the body is not made up of one part, but of
many . . . there are many parts but one body.

1 Corinthians 12:14

When Paul talked about the church being the body of Christ and all of us individual parts of that body, it reminds me of a recipe. So many varying ingredients to make a particular dish – ingredients which on their own can be pretty unappetising but once blended together become one glorious, indivisible taste. The psalmist said 'O taste and see that the Lord is Good.' Lord, I have tasted, here I am, just one more individual, an insignificant ingredient waiting to be stirred and blended into your indissoluble body.

> *One body we, one body who partakes*
> *One church united in communion blest;*
> *One name we bear, one bread of life we break*
> *With all the saints on earth and saints at rest.*
> *One with each other, Lord, for one in Thee*
> *Who art one Saviour and one Living Head.*

George W. Briggs

17th September

The Lord turned and looked straight at Peter.

Luke 22:61

Sometimes words aren't necessary – silence and the meeting of eyes hold complete meaning. Charles Wesley, in one of the 6,000 or so hymns he wrote, said, 'Pity from thine eye let fall, by a look my soul recall.' Not many of us are impressed by long, theological lectures, but the eyes of a starving child, or joy in the eyes of a terminally ill patient, have direct contact with our hearts. Contact . . . Lord, I look at pictures, artists' impressions of Your suffering . . . I look to make visual contact with God made Man and to seek spiritual contact with Your love.

'I looked on Him: He looked on me, and we were one for ever.'

C. H. Spurgeon

18th September

Jesus answered, 'I tell you the truth, you are looking for me, not because you saw miraculous signs
but because you ate the loaves and had your fill.'

John 6:26

Forgive me, Lord, that too often I come in prayer because I'm after
something – you know my weakness, You look right into my
heart and You see my motives before I realise them myself. Thank
You for all the blessings of this day, the miraculous signs of Your
love and mercy, the coal in the bunker, the bread in the bread-bin,
the petrol in the car . . . I have enough for my body and physical
comfort but I need to come now to pray for the food for my
soul . . . the Bread of Life.

> *Break Thou the bread of life, O Lord to me,*
> *As Thou didst break the loaves beside the sea;*
> *Beyond the sacred page I seek Thee Lord,*
> *My spirit pants for Thee, O living word.*

Mary A. Lathbury

19th September

A man reaps what he sows.

Galatians 6:7

A hobby is therapeutic in all sorts of ways – it gives us something
else to think about above daily routine, brings us fresh faces and
gives satisfaction a relaxation. William Gill's hobby was collecting folk tunes – he worked for the post office – and it's thanks to
him that we have the beautiful Manx tune set to the hymn he
wrote, 'Hear us O Lord from heaven, Thy dwelling place'. It is a
hymn which encompasses the thought of harvests with our daily
need for God's word. I can see, Lord, that if I'm going to be
ill-tempered, bitter and fault-finding I shall only reap loneliness . . . help me today to sow seeds of love.

Sow in our hearts the seeds of Thy dear love,
That we may reap contentment, joy and peace.

William Henry Gill

20th September

With all my resources I have provided for the
Temple of my God gold, silver, bronze, iron, wood,
onyx, turquoise, fine stone and marble.

1 Chronicles 29:2

As far as King David was concerned only the best was good
enough to be used in the temple building and he chose mineral
treasures to beautify the Holy place. And what a fantastic sight
our Holy places can be, whether a cathedral in Venice with
man-adorned artistry or natural cathedrals such as in the Cheddar
Caves. There are buildings all around me, but I hardly ever notice
them, I don't really look at the stone, bricks and timber of shops,
factories, schools, offices, churches . . . yet every building, Lord,
however grand or ugly, is made from Your materials – thank you
for Your rich providence in the harvest from the ground.

Praise God for the Harvest that comes from the ground,
By drill or by mineshaft, by opencast mine;
For oil and for iron, for copper and coal,
Praise God, who in love, has provided them all.

Brian A. Wren

21st September

So Eli told Samuel, 'Go and lie down and if He calls
you say, "Speak, Lord, for Your servant is listening." '

1 Samuel 3:9

My mind is bombarded with voices . . . distraction . . . noise –
traffic, places, children, dogs, machines . . . there are times when I
can't hear You, Lord – times when I'm not listening either, so

wrapped up in things there is no room for the voice of God. Lord, help me to break this 'hamster-in-a-wheel' mentality, teach me how to listen, keenly, like I do when I'm really interested and involved; open my cluttered mind to Your call . . . speak to me, Lord.

> *O give me Samuel's mind*
> *A sweet unmurmering faith*
> *Obedient and resigned to Thee in life and death,*
> *That I might read with childlike eyes,*
> *Truths that are hidden from the wise.*
>
> John Drummond Burns

22nd September

> They devoted themselves to the apostles' teaching
> and to the fellowship, to the breaking of bread and
> to prayer.
>
> *Acts 2:42*

Lord, help me realise the importance of fellowship during the week – one Sunday dinner per week would leave my body hungry and one or two hours of worship per week will keep my soul hungry and undernourished. Give me a true sense of belonging around Your table and a deep need to pray for and with others. Bless our togetherness, I pray, and may Your church on earth thrive on the fundamentals of scripture, communion and prayer.

> *Let us break bread together with the Lord,*
> *Let us praise God together in the Lord,*
> *When I fall on my knees*
> *With my face to the rising sun,*
> *O, Lord, have mercy on me.*
>
> Negro spiritual

23rd September

'But Lord,' Gideon asked, 'how can I save Israel
. . . I am the least in my family.'

Judges 6:15

A young man stood before a group of Gideons to give his testimony. Some years before he had brutally raped and murdered a Christian girl of just 21; he was caught, convicted and sentenced to a long period in jail. He had served eighteen months when two Gideons visited him, gave him a Bible and told him that a certain woman was praying for him. The young man rejected the Bible and the men left – they were totally surprised to be called back to his cell some weeks later to find this vile murderer had been brought to his knees before the Lord . . . the knowledge that his victim's mother was praying for him had pierced his heart and he wanted to be accepted by such a love that made her action possible. Lord, of all, the good and innocent and the cheats, rapists and murderers, I bring in prayer today all the international band of Gideons and the lives who find Jesus through the Bibles they leave in hospitals, prisons, hotels, colleges, and planes.

An Auxiliary told my wife and I how thrilled she was when she emerged from a doctor's waiting room, having placed her first Gideon Bible there 'I praised the Lord,' she said, 'to think that it was something I had been able to do for Him.'

Darryl Brown
past national vice-pres. of Gideon Society

24th September

Jesus said, 'But I tell you that anyone who is angry
with his brother will be subject to judgement.'

Matthew 5:21

How is it that a day can be perfectly pleasant . . . everything going along swimmingly, then wham! twenty seconds from one person and the whole day turns sour, perhaps even the week, even, if we allow it, our lives. Lord, some people in particular annoy me almost beyond endurance . . . I feel angry right inside. What can I do about it? When tempers flare may I feel Your spirit of calm, help me to see the futility of anger which festers away, day after day, eating away at my life and spoiling my present . . . help me, Lord, to turn to You, turn away from the person who provokes these feelings and look to Jesus who forbids my sin.

Christ is the world's Peace, He and no other;
No one can serve Him and despise his brother.

Fred Pratt Green

25th September

A man from Bethlehem, together with his wife and
two sons, went to live for a while in the country of
Moab.

Ruth 1

All sorts of reasons take us away from the place of our birth; parents, jobs, college, university, marriage, search for a job, promotion, voluntary service overseas . . . every reason brings with it the challenge of new friends and strange surroundings . . . fear of unfamiliar customs and faces and currency. Lord, I'm not very good at uprooting myself; if I have to move, help me to face it all calmly and give me courage to join in with new surroundings and clubs. I pray for all those who are starting life somewhere different, for students, refugees or those entering sheltered accommodation or residential homes. Wherever I go, Lord, I need not worry for You are with me, closer than breathing.

And it's from the old I travel to the new —
Keep me travelling along with You.

Sydney Carter

26th September

Come let us bow down in worship, let us kneel
before the Lord our Maker.

Psalm 95:6

Many of us have childhood memories of bed-time prayers . . .
kneeling eyes tightly shut, speaking to Jesus in best whispers.
There is something special about the act of kneeling in prayer, of
actually getting down on our knees and shutting out the world
. . . after all it's the same Jesus we are speaking to as listened to us
all those years ago – He must feel sad that old habits get tossed
aside with maturity, forgotten in all the business of our lives.
Lord, I kneel today, I seek to recapture the awe and wonder and
reverence I once felt . . . teach me how to pray all over again.

*The time of business does not with me differ from the time of
prayer, and in the noise and clatter of my kitchen, while several
persons are at the same time calling for different things, I possess
God in as great tranquillity as if I were upon my knees at the
blessed sacrament.*

Brother Lawrence

27th September

Jesus said to them: 'bring some of the fish you have
just caught.' Simon Peter climbed aboard and
dragged the net ashore – it was full of large fish.

John 21:10

The incredible variety of fish in the oceans is so enormous that
even today there are still new discoveries being made. We feed
happily from the shining, teeming netfulls of fish the fishermen
bring ashore in the great trawlers and container vessels; the riches,
beauty and harvest of the sea is for the most part untapped. Lord,
such a bountiful planet, two thirds oceans and seas with fish,
corals, constant tides and currents . . . a vast underwater world
beyond our imaginings. Thank You for the food from the sea, and
thank You that by television pictures I can glimpse a tiny part of

the secrets below the waves.

> *The ocean deeps, the currents and tides,*
> *The diatons, the fishes, and the whale,*
> *The storm, the reef, the waterspout, the calm,*
> *Praise and reflect the wonder of Christ.*

J. P. McAuley

28th September

I will lie down and sleep in peace.

Psalm 4:8

It doesn't matter who we are, Queen, president of the local W.I., single parent or international opera star – we must have our sleep. We need rest and peace in our sleep, not fitful churnings that leave us dark-eyed and shattered in the morning . . . there is nothing more horrible than nights of tension, worry and fear. O Lord, You promised Your peace in our hearts . . . a peace that cannot be found anywhere but in Your loving presence. I pray for that peace now, and I pray for the blessing of a good night's rest.

Now may the Lord of peace Himself give you peace at all times and in every way. The Lord be with all of you.

2 Thessalonians 3:16

29th September

Jesus said, 'But go and learn what this means, 'I desire mercy, not sacrifice.'

Matthew 9:13

Jesus quoted the prophet Hosea (6:6) when He said this to the cynical pharisees. The wise old 'forth-tellers' of God's message in the Old Testament were always hammering away against injustice, double-standards and religious hypocrisy; Jesus Himself underlined this call to worship the Living God with our entire being, in words, thoughts and actions. Lord, forgive me if my worship has been hollow, rigid . . . a ritual observance for social display . . . so fill my being that my life will be a witness of mercy and justice for the sake of Jesus Christ.

Hear the word of the Lord: 'the multitude of your sacrifices – what are they to me?' says the Lord, 'stop bringing meaningless offerings! Stop doing wrong, learn to do right!'

Isaiah 1 11/13/16

30th September

'My dear brothers, take note of this: everyone should be quick to listen, slow to speak and slow to become angry.'

James 1:19

I've been at it again, Lord . . . I've been slow to listen, quick to open my mouth and ultra-speedy in losing my temper! I'm slow to take advice because of the pride that tells me I know best; I lose my temper because things don't fall into place as I want . . . Heavenly Father, help me to get myself sorted out – to have the grace not to let situations get out of hand and the humility to learn that there are others in the community as well as me. I pray today for a listening ear . . . patience in conversation and good humour.

> *Let me in Thy strength subdue*
> *Evil tempers, words untrue;*
> *Thoughts impure and deeds unkind*
> *All things hateful to Thy mind.*

Whitfield G. Wills

1st October

Rejoice in the Lord, always; I will say it again, Rejoice.'

Philippians 4:4

Just at the moment I don't feel like rejoicing. Surely, it's impossible anyway to be able to rejoice all the time . . . it's not normal. When Paul spoke about rejoicing, though, he was in prison! A former pharisee, belittled and persecuted, suffering hostility and loss of freedom . . . and writing about rejoicing. Can knowing Jesus as a personal Saviour make so much difference? Oh, yes it can! Lord, lift me out of myself and may my whole attitude today be one of straightforward rejoicing for all that I have and for all that You mean to me.

Always joyful, Lord? It's not easy to accept . . .
I just have to try to work it out.
Help me to rejoice in the people I know,
They aren't perfect, but neither am I.
Let me know, beyond doubt, that You will never go away,
And whether things are easy or tough, let me know through my
laughter and tears — You are with me: and there's the Joy.

Eddie Askew

2nd October

Remember how the Lord your God led you all the
way.

Deuteronomy 8:2

Looking back over my life I see many occasions when cross-roads were reached . . . times when I worried about the decisions I had to make, yet now, in the way my life has knitted into the pattern of other lives and situations, I see the guiding hand of the Lord. I remember good times and downright awful times, times of praise and times of depression and doubt, but through all, when my vision was clouded and my mind puzzled, my life was led and preserved by the unseen presence. Lord, I remember . . . and I'm grateful.

All the way my Saviour leads me: what have I to ask beside?
Can I doubt His tender mercy, who through life had been my
Guide:
Heavenly peace, divinest comfort, here by faith in Him to dwell;
For I know whate'er befall me, Jesus doeth all things well.

Fanny J. Crosby

3rd October

Dear friends, let us love one another, for love
comes from God . . . God is Love.

1 John 4:7/8

Our world has more than its fair share of unlovable people – nasty
types who smuggle drugs, spies, violent robbers, men within both
unions and management who determinedly keep the pot of distrust and mutual dislike boiling . . . we could make a huge list of
the people we would not care to find living next-door to us.
However, if we are to be true followers of Jesus, if we accept and
believe with all our hearts that God is Love, then there should be
no room for lists of 'desirables' and 'undesirables' . . . in our
dealings with people we should treat them all with the touch of
our Saviour. But, Lord, it's easier said than done: like Peter I am
finding it hard to get to grips with the fact that I mustn't call
anybody or anything You have created inferior or unclean, or
unlovable. Help me, Lord, to love people in Your name.

*People think there are circumstances when one may deal with
human beings without love, but no such circumstances ever exist.
Inanimate objects may be dealt with without love: we may fell
trees, break bricks, hammer iron without love. But human beings
cannot be handled without Love.*

L. N. Tolstoy

4th October

You crown the year with Your bounty, the
meadows are covered with flocks, and the valleys
are mantled with grain: they shout for joy and sing.

Psalm 65:11/13

Once more the Harvest is safely gathered . . . we've fought off the
carrot-fly, the mildew and rust, in some cases the club-root and
caterpillars have been victorious, but over all, the harvest is good.
I love the smell of stored apples, the sight of silos brim full of
grain . . . I am full of praise and thanksgiving as I stand at the
crown of the year and consider all the harvest from the land for
mankind. How can I say thank You, without sounding trite . . .

words feel inadequate . . . perhaps the best way of praising is to have a wonderful time, enjoy and share our good gifts.

> *Now the year is crowned with blessing*
> *As we gather in the grain;*
> *And, our grateful thanks expressing*
> *Loud we raise a joyous strain.*

Ellen Thorneycroft Fowler

5th October

Some men came to Jesus bringing to Him a paralytic.

Mark 2:3

The wonderful lesson to be learnt from this story in Mark's gospel is that Jesus can use anyone, whatever their circumstances, for His glory. Too often the disabled in our midst are down-graded, not given adequate opportunities or importance . . . we don't expect a great deal from them. Yet the paralytic who was useless to others, was invaluable to Jesus. Every so often I come across greeting cards and calendars painted by artists who use their feet or mouth: when given the opportunity these disabled people leave us standing by their dedication and enthusiasm. Lord, I ask that I can gather with my friends not to compete, but to be used as valuable individuals . . . stretch me and stretch my friends so that we learn to lean more on You.

Although it may seem God is being grossly unfair and is giving us a heavier cross to bear, we really don't know what the person next-door has to live with. God is doing in each one of our lives something expressly different than He is doing in another's.

Joni Earekson

6th October

. . . 'I know that it is my fault . . .'

Jonah 1:12

Jonah was no stirring, charismatic figure, no tower of righteousness – he was a coward, a defeatist and quick-tempered with it. But he was honest. There's a saying that there is good in the worst of us and evil in the best of us . . . so we must not condemn old Jonah – he was honest enough to own up that he was running away from God so it had to be his fault that the dreadful storm had blown up. He was brave too, because he knew his honesty would cost him his life . . . the terrified sailors picked him up and heaved him into the sea! So, Jonah was honest, brave and finally obedient . . . suddenly he sounds more like a prophet, I wish I could use all the three words to describe me, Lord . . . days would run much more smoothly if more people were prepared to accept responsibility, live honestly and obey God.

This almighty God, who created heaven and earth, who is so high above us that we can barely begin to grasp who He is, promises that every wound, every fault, every sin will be dealt with with tenderness and compassion.

Delia Smith

7th October

Jesus went up into the hills to pray.

Matthew 14:23

Just imagine the clamour for Jesus – the great teacher, the miraculous healer – the countryside must have been crawling with people crying out for the Master's touch, His blessing, His smile . . . a never ending press of needy people. How Jesus must have longed to escape to the hills. Lord, You understand stress, the demands that came drag us down . . . I long just to have a short time of peace, just long enough so that I can get back to home and job with renewed vigour. Today, I seek a place of quiet . . . I need it to think and to pray and then to live again.

While here we kneel upon the mount of prayer,
The plough lies waiting in the furrow there:
Here we sought God that we might know His will,
There we must do it, serve Him, seek Him still.

Samuel Greg

8th October

Whether you turn to the right or to the left, your
ears will hear a voice behind you saying: 'This is the
Way, walk in it.'

Isaiah 30:21

I need guidance, today, Lord. I feel hesitant and a bit confused
about the way ahead. I'm not sure what to do so I wait to feel Your
reassurance . . . like a sheep out on the moor I shall have to be led
by my shepherd. Lead me, Lord, for I do not know the way . . .
You know my need . . . I don't want to use words now . . . I'm
just going to listen for Your divine guidance, trust You and follow
You.

Jesus answered: I am the Way and the Truth and the Life.

John 14:6

9th October

. . . You have forsaken your first love. Remember
the height from which you have fallen!

Revelation 2:4

Lord, I feel ashamed when I look back at 'special' times, when in
the first flush of commitment I was ablaze with enthusiasm for the
gospel, I was eager for Bible Study, truly hungry to grow in faith.
Life becomes a long, rough haul with more downs than ups for
most of us . . . show me, Lord, that it was the same for the
prophets, the disciples, and all Your followers through the centuries . . . what I need is endurance – to find again the love that
knows no end, the love that always hopes and always perseveres
in joy.

> *Where is the blessedness I knew*
> *When first I saw the Lord:*
> *Where is that soul-refreshing view*
> *Of Jesus and His word.*

William Cowper

10th October

Share with God's people who are in need.

Romans 12:12

Somerset Maughan wrote a haunting story about a man who won a vast amount of money – how his family disintegrated and turned against him because he chose to share his money and his house. His whole lifestyle falls apart, people he tries to help take advantage of him and his high ideals are thrown in his face. It's a hard tale with a hint to the reader that good intentions of sharing are all very well, but firstly, we don't really intend to share everything, and secondly, it never works out anyway. O Lord, I can be moderately generous – a couple of times a year – can I ever get to grips with practical, Christ-like sharing?

> *Then let the servant church arise*
> *A caring church that longs to be*
> *A partner in Christ's sacrifice*
> *And clothed in Christ's humanity.*
> *For He alone whose blood was shed*
> *Can cure the fever in our blood;*
> *And teach us how to share our bread*
> *And feed the starving multitude.*

Fred Pratt Green

11th October

A man reaps what he sows. The one who sows to
please his sinful nature will reap destruction, the
one who sows to please the Spirit will reap eternal
life.

Galatians 6:7

Lord, I offer You the harvest of my life. I cannot go back over the year to hurriedly sow some extra seeds where my harvest is looking patchy – it's too late . . . I cannot return to spring-time to exchange my 'oats' for 'barley' – it's too late, my seed was chosen and now the crop has grown. So here I stand with the fruits of my experience – not quite what I'd hoped for, neither in quantity nor quality, but it's all I have . . . me. Lord, have mercy.

Even so, Lord, quickly come,
Bring Thy final harvest home;
Gather Thou Thy people in
Free from sorrow, free from sin . . .
Come, with all Thine angels, come,
Raise the glorious Harvest Home.

Henry Alford

12th October

'Therefore, I can tell you, her many sins have been
forgiven, for she loved much. But he who has been
forgiven little, loves little.'

Luke 8:47

During an international tour speaking on the power of God's love
and forgiveness, Corrie Ten Boon suddenly came face to face with
a former guard from her days in Ravensbruck. She recognised him
as having been the most cruel and evil man; he held out his hand to
her . . . she felt unable to take it, but prayed desperately for God's
forgiveness. In that strength she was able to clasp the man's hand.
Lord, in the light of the sufferings of the concentration camps the
trivial little things I'm called on to forgive seem absurd . . . yet
even so, I am grudging and slow to forgive.

In blazing light Your cross reveals
The truth we dimly knew;
How small the debts men owe to us,
How great our debt to You.

Rosamond E. Herklots

13th October

The soul who sins is the one who will die. The son
will not share the guilt of the father, nor will the
father share the guilt of the son.

Ezekiel 18:20

In the language we understand today, the prophet Ezekiel was saying: 'with God, you can't pass the buck!' The Israelites were steeped in the belief that a person's misfortune was because of sin, if not theirs then it must have been their father's sin. It was a lovely way to get rid of personal guilt! Ezekiel, however, told them that their God had other ideas and that it was no good to think that they could dodge responsibility for their personal sin. Lord, it is so tempting to blame others and excuse ourselves – help me to face up to the consequences of my actions and words . . . my sin is nothing to do with anybody but me . . . Father forgive, my guilty soul.

> *Me for Thine own Thou love'st to take,*
> *In time and in eternity;*
> *Thou never, never wilt forsake,*
> *A helpless soul that trust in Thee.*

Charles Wesley

14th October

For the message of the cross is foolishness to those
who are perishing, but to us who are being saved, it
is the power of God.

1 Corinthians 1:18

A great deal of motivation can be summed up in the phrase 'what's in it for me?' It may sound cynical, but it is a fact of our life that human nature is always more willing when there is reward attached to the action. So to the majority of people the cross of Jesus is a stumbling block, because they see in it only failure . . . agony . . . even a waste of time . . . foolishness . . . they can see no advantage in the cross whatsoever. Lord, I kneel to proclaim that the cross is central to my faith – to me it means Your consummate act of Love towards me. It demonstrates Your almighty power to overcome death and bring all believers into the glory of eternal life.

Think nothing too little; seek for the Cross in the daily incidents of life; look for the Cross in everything. Nothing is too little which relates to man's salvation, nor is there anything too little in which either to please God or to serve Satan.

E. B. Pusey

15th October

Solomon had four thousand stalls for chariot
horses and twelve thousand horses.

1 Kings 4:26

Horses have a secure place in people's hearts from the elegant horses of the Household Cavalry to the solid old shire horses gleaming with brasses and harness at a rural show. Viewers sit on the edge of their seats at the Horse of the Year Show, and the pet pony is lavished with an affection seldom given to anything else. . . . Yes, horses are part of our heritage and part of our culture. . . . Today, Lord, I want to give thanks for the way horses are used to give pleasure and confidence to disabled riders – thank You for the care and dedication of the instructors and helpers in this heart-warming association.

> *What is the creature's skill or force?*
> *The sprightly man or war-like horse,*
> *The piercing wit, the active limb,*
> *All are to mean delights for Him.*

Isaac Watts

16th October

'Lo, I am with you always, even unto the end of the
age.'

Matthew 25:28

This promise Jesus made has brought comfort to all His believers when they grasp the almighty wonder of its meaning. Of course I want You with me always, Lord, but I tend to forget You in the launderette, in the dentist's chair or rushing to collect the children. My mind has condensed Your power to fit my understanding . . . I have unconsciously confined Your presence to 'nice' places and 'appropriate' times. Treated You like a visiting V.I.P., the best cups brought out and the floorcloth out of sight. Lord of my life, Lord of today, give me the insight to know Your presence anywhere and everywhere.

Christ in Woolworth's – I did not think to find You there –
crucifixes large and small . . . sixpence and three pence, on a tray
among the artificial pearls, paste rings, tin watches, beads of glass.
It seemed so strange to find You there – fingered by people coarse
and cross who had no reverence at all. Yet, what is it You would
say? 'For these I hung upon my cross,' Dear Lord, forgive such
fools as I who thought it strange to find You there – when You are
with us everywhere.

Teresa Hooley

17th October

My people are fools. They do not know me . . .they
are skilled in doing evil, they do not know how to
do good.

Jeremiah 4:22

The prophet Jeremiah cried out in anguish for the way the
Israelites had forgotten their God . . . turned their backs on the
One who had brought them out of captivity, the One who would
give to the nation a Redeemer, their omission of prayer and
worship led eventually to the sins of apathy and rejection. Lord,
show me that just in the same way a tiger cub can be cuddled and
controlled, then as it grows it becomes too wild to handle, in the
same way my sins grow from easy to handle to choking evil. I too
can be a fool and skilled in doing what is wrong . . . Lord, I long
to return to Your ways and do good.

The fool says in his heart
'There is no God. . . . '
The Lord looks down from heaven on the sons of men to see if
there are any who seek God.

Psalm 53:1/2

18th October

There is neither Jew nor Greek, slave nor free, male
nor female, for you are all one in Christ Jesus.

Galatians 3:28

Two human noises defy racial identification – they are weeping and laughter. It looks sometimes as though Governments of this world go out of their way to highlight the differences between people . . . to maintain fear, suspicion and separation. I thank my God that in Jesus Christ, all barriers are broken down, we are made one in His love – He doesn't care if I am black, deformed, yellow, a peasant, a marquis, young or ancient – Jesus loves me as I am. Lord, help me strive for the unity of the precious world in Your name.

> *As Christ breaks bread and bids us share*
> *Each proud division ends;*
> *The love that made us makes us one,*
> *And strangers now are friends.*

Brian A. Wren

19th October

Jesus said, 'do not worry about tomorrow, each
day has enough trouble of its own.'

Matthew 6:34

It's just impossible for me not to worry about tomorrow. . . . Someone said: today is the tomorrow you were worried about yesterday! Oh the wasted energy on panic, the wasted speculation and headaches, Lord, why don't I read Your Holy word? Even though it's Monday I shall make a positive decision to live in today – to enjoy today – and before I go to sleep tonight, I will give thanks for the completeness of today and leave tomorrow for the morning.

> *Lord, for tomorrow and its needs*
> *I do not pray;*
> *But keep me, guide me, hold me Lord,*
> *Just for today.*

Anon

20th October

The Lord said to Ananias: 'Go on your way for this
man is my chosen instrument.'

Acts 9:15

Ananias must have been stunned! Fancy God telling him that the
maniac Saul of Tarsus, the man hell-bent on obliterating the
Christians . . . this Saul was God's chosen instrument – Ananias
may have been dumbfounded, probably mistrustful and
frightened too, but he had the faith to obey his Lord. If only I had
that same faith not to rely on my own intuition and conclusions,
but to be able to say with conviction, as the founder of the Red
Cross declared: All men are brothers. So help me Lord, to live and
work alongside my brothers and sisters . . . for all I know they
may be Your chosen instruments, too.

*I am born to serve You, to be Yours, to be Your instrument. Let
me be Your blind instrument. I ask not to see – I ask not to know –
I ask simply to be used.*

J. H. Newman

21st October

Peter said to Jesus, 'We have left all we have to
follow You.'

Luke 18:28

Today, Lord I want to think about men and women who, many
years ago, left all they knew, their secure, familiar things of home
to take the message of the Risen Jesus into far-flung corners of the
world. They gave their youth, sometimes their health, even for
some they gave back to You children, wives and husbands . . .
working to exhaustion, serving, sowing seeds which are now
yielding the vigorous fruit of Your growing church in China, in
South America and Africa. Your loyal servants, Lord, who gave
up their own lives so that others would be loved into Your
Kingdom; may their faith inspire and move me today.

As of old apostles heard it,
By the Galilean lake;
turned from home and toil and kindred,
Leaving all for His dear sake.

Cecil Frances Alexander

22nd October

An argument started among the disciples as to
which of them would be the greatest.

Luke 9:46

It just goes to show how ordinary the disciples were, even though
they were witnessing the most astounding miracles, listening daily
to soul-searching words from their Master . . . on top of all this
they sat around nit-picking about which of them was the most
important. Show me, Lord, how prone to pettiness we all are,
however high-minded and well-intentioned we like to feel. Save
me from the creeping sin of pride . . . let me put Jesus Christ in the
position of greatest importance, now and for always.

Christ is our advocate on high,
Thou art our advocate within;
O plead the truth and make reply
To every argument of sin.

Alfred H. Vine

23rd October

When they had sung a hymn they went out to the
Mount of Olives.

Matthew 26:30

Seems strange to think of Jesus singing a hymn . . . on the other
hand it shouldn't be strange because singing is part of worship
and Jesus was a worshipping Jew. Forgive me, Lord, that I don't
use my imagination enough in the right channels – it never occurs

to me to think of Jesus singing yet when I'm supposed to be singing hymns my mind can carry too many drifting thoughts . . . thank You, Lord for the lovely poems, hymns, psalms, songs and music which thrills me, which lifts my heart in praise, which make me feel brighter and happier.

Think of a world without any poetry,
Think of a book without any words,
Think of a song without any music
Think of a hymn without any verse;
We thank You Lord for poetry and music
We thank You Lord and praise Your holy name.

Doreen Newport

24th October

God said to Jonah: 'Do you have a right to be angry with the vine?' 'I do,' said Jonah, 'I am angry enough to die.'

Jonah 4:9

Jonah's petulance is reminiscent of the child who yells in tantrum: 'I'll scream and scream and scream until I'm sick.' In Jonah's pouting, 'I'm angry enough to die,' we can see him stamp his foot. I know I have no right to throw my weight around, no right to indulge in being angry, but there are times when I get so worked up, that I'm determined to be angry. Open my eyes, Lord to the stupidity of my temper, show me that nothing is achieved by anger, and no-one is hurt but me.

In your anger do not sin. Do not let the sun go down while you are still angry, and do not give the devil a foothold. . . .

Ephesians 4:26/27

25th October

They will be like a well-watered garden.

Jeremiah 31:12

1976 was the year of serious summer drought, parched roadside verges, dried-up river beds, burnt lawns and the unfamiliar sights of withered plants. During that time I visited a model village which has its own stream running straight through the middle. There, amidst a toasted landscape was a patch of vivid green; well-watered, lush and thriving. O Lord, I claim the promise that all who come to You will be like a well-watered garden, fresh and full of spiritual vitality in a sin-dry world.

> I come to the garden alone
> While the dew is still on the roses
> And the voice I hear, falling on my ear,
> The Son of God discloses;
> And He walks with me and He talks with me
> And He tells me I am His own.

C. Austin Miles

26th October

Jesus said: 'Be on your guard against all kinds of greed; a man's life does not consist in the abundance of his possessions.'

Luke 12:15

The great and powerful Emperor of China who ordered the building of the Great Wall of China, the building so vast it is the only man-made object visible from space, was petrified of death. Materially he had everything but he had no peace of mind. The owner of a dozen Van Dycks or Picasso's has theoretical millions yet while he keeps them, he has nothing more in his life than canvas and oils. The more we acquire, the more we want . . . we go on a spiralling ego-trip yet fail to capture peace of mind. The greatest spiritual lives have been uncluttered by possessions, Jesus had no home, Lord, help me to get things in perspective and to value people more than possessions.

Put to death, therefore, whatever belongs to your earthly nature, sexual immorality, impurity, lust, evil desires and greed which is idolatory.

Colossians 3:5

27th October

Each man has his own gift from God; one has this
gift, another has that.

1 Corinthians 7:7

In other words, never say you have nothing to offer – don't feel
dismayed that there is no part for you to play – you have! No one
is too young nor too old, too inexperienced too tired . . . God's
Holy word declares that everyone has been given a gift and, even
better, we all have something different to offer. Some are meticu-
lous organisers while others have the gift to encourage, again
others can go into a home and chat or help with the washing . . .
there is a place for choirmaster, organist, gardener, cleaner,
preacher and visitor; and a great need for those who will pray.
Lord, I may not be able to give an organ recital but I can pray . . .
help me to use the gift You have given me.

> *My talents, gifts and graces, Lord*
> *Into Thy blessed hands receive . . .*
> *My every sacred moment spend,*
> *In publishing the Sinners' Friend.*

Charles Wesley

28th October

But Jael, Heber's wife, picked up a tent peg and a
hammer and went quietly to Sisera while he lay fast
asleep. She drove the peg though his temple into the
ground, and he died.

Judges 4:21

Accounts of violence today make me feel physically sick.
Violence to little babies, taken to hospital with cigarette burns,
the brutality of muggings on frail old people, the indiscriminate
violence in crowds – how can human beings behave like it
towards other human beings? It doesn't take long to realise that
human nature has always been vile . . . the Bible gives horrific
accounts of violence – Jesus my Lord died at the hands of violent

men. I can only pray for these people and for their victims and beg You Lord, to change their sick and wicked hearts.

The boy's eyes were narrowed with hate. He started towards me and I stepped back as the knife whizzed by my stomach. Suddenly, it felt as though the hand of God grabbed my arm . . . I could picture myself just a few weeks before standing in the dark street, trying to kill an enemy.

Nicky Cruz

29th October

'You are the light of the world. A city on a hill cannot be hidden.'

Matthew 5:14

It's a lovely sight to see a distant town twinkling invitingly in the darkness – there is a warmth and reassurance in the lights that tell us other people are up and about as well – we are not alone – there are others packing lunches for the morning, comforting a sick child, getting on with ironing, watching the television . . . Lord, as I look at the lights of a town or city, I remember that the church should have the same inviting glow for souls in a dark and lonely world. Your church; the collective body of Your people . . . Father, I cannot hide the light of Your love in my home.

O word of God incarnate, O wisdom from on high;
Truth unchanged, unchanging, O light of our dark sky;
We praise Thee for the radiance
That from the hallowed page
A lantern to our footsteps shines on from age to age.

William W. How

30th October

You anoint me head with oil, my cup overflows,
Surely goodness and love will follow me all the
days of my life.

Psalm 23:5/6

Reservoirs are such tranquil, beautiful places . . . it gives endless inspiration to tired minds, to boating enthusiasts, artists and fishermen. Walking one day over the dam of the local reservoir brought the words of Psalm 23 to mind as I watched the water cascading down the overflow and away into the stream below. Relentless gallons of water, yet the reservoir remained full. To those who come to Jesus, whose cups overflow, there will be granted a never-ending supply of 'living water' . . . a cup overflowing with so many blessings to share – thank You, Lord that Your reservoir of Love will never run dry.

My head Thou dost with oil anoint,
And my cup overflows.

William Whittingham

31st October

A priest happened to be going down the same road
and when he saw the man he passed by on the other
side.

Luke 10:31

In a car-park I noticed a young girl with her boy-friend. I was with a friend and as we neared the young couple I could see that the boy was sprawled on the tarmac, being sick into a drain. We knew them by sight – felt instantly embarrassed and sorry for them, and we passed by. In that split second needed to decide whether to help or not, we hesitated and walked on. Lord, forgive me the sin of cold rejection . . . of bothering more about myself than someone in distress . . . have mercy on me . . . miserable, selfish me.

Pass me not O gentle Saviour
Hear my humble cry
And while others Thou art calling
Do not pass me by.

1st November

To all in Rome who are loved by God and called to
be saints. . . .

Romans 1:7

We tend to think of a saint as someone who no longer lives on this earth – or secondly, the mental picture sees a man or woman of incredible age . . . someone whose austere sanctity lifts them out of the reach of ordinary people. Saint . . . Halo etc. Lord, help me to dispel this line of thought – saints are those who live close to You and by so doing brightening lives around them in the pool of Your Love. . . . There are saints down the road, in the cottage hospital, in the school for the maladjusted, on the end of a Samaritan telephone; thank You Lord, for saintly lives which now and again touch mine – they are a beacon; may I learn from them more of Jesus.

For all the saints who from their labours rest,
Who Thee by faith before the world confessed;
Thy name, O Jesus, be for ever blest,
Alleluia!

William W. How

2nd November

I, the Lord have called you in righteousness, I will
take hold of your hand, I will keep you. . . .

Isaiah 42:6

Frances Ridley Havergal, the Victorian hymn-writer was only 43 when she died. In her last days she found great peace in listening to her favourite Bible passages read to her and the forty second chapter of Isaiah was especially meaningful to her. At verse 6 she stopped the reader and whispered, 'called, held, kept . . . and used'. Frances knew her Lord had called her, had held her in His keeping and even though her life was so short, He had wonderfully used her to spread the news of Jesus Christ to young women in particular. Today, Lord, I pray that somehow, somewhere, You will be able to use me, too.

In our joys and in our sorrows
Days of toil and hours of ease,
Still He calls, in cares and pleasures,
That we love Him more than these.

Cecil Francis Alexander

3rd November

Wash and perfume yourself – and put on your best clothes.

Ruth 3:3

Sunday is a lovely day! Time to relax in a deep, hot bath – soothing, refreshing . . . it takes years away from us! We spruce up and feel new people, a good sprinkle of talc or perfume and we feel ready to face the world once more. Lord, if that is how I feel when my body is washed and attended to, how much better, happier and healthier will I feel in my heart if I ask Jesus to wash away my sins – that will roll the cares away too and make me a new person in Christ – then not only will I be able to face the world, but I shall be able to share with the world the saving grace of my living Lord . . . every day will be a happier day!

Happy Day, Happy Day,
When Jesus washed my sins away;
He taught me how to watch and pray
And live rejoicing every day,
Happy Day, Happy Day,
When Jesus washed my sins away.

Philip Doddridge

4th November

Blessed is the man who fears the Lord....
He will have no fear of bad news.

Psalm 112:1/7

News! 95% of the news churned out via television, radio and
newspapers could well be headlined: 'suffering'. Relentless and
heartbreaking stories of inner-city dereliction, disease, civil war
... an earthquake here and a hurricane there – child abuse,
murder, cruelty to animals ... on and on, day after day. Show me
Lord, that it won't help to bury my head in the pillow – may I
realise that Christians have a counter-offensive to all the world's
horror – Jesus Christ Lives: the best news of all time.

> *Spread the good news o'er all the earth,*
> *Jesus had died and has risen –*
> *Alleluia, Alleluia, give thanks to the Risen Lord,*
> *Alleluia, Alleluia, give praise to His name.*

Don Fishel

5th November

Hear this word you cows of Bashan ... you
women who oppress the poor and crush the
needy....

Amos 4:1

In the Old Testament we get accustomed to the treachery, deceit
and vile goings on amongst men – but here are words to make us
do a double take: the prophet Amos was sounding off at the deep
end about women, and especially those who abused their status
and power. Amos was a true social reformer – he cared passion-
ately about the injustice he saw in the society and he stood up
boldly, in the strength of his God to condemn what he saw. Some
two and a half thousand years later the same exploitation continues – women have the capability to outmaneouvre men in their
deceit, their lust for power and status. O Lord, I pray for some of
Amos' commitment and justice ... let me be afraid of no-one –

man or woman in the search for truth, peace and freedom.

On just and unjust Thou Thy care dost freely shower:
Make us, Thy children, free from greed and lust for power;
Lest human justice, yoked with man's unequal laws,
Oppress the needy and neglect the humble cause.

G. B. Caird

6th November

Jesus said: 'The spirit is willing but the flesh is
weak.'

Matthew 26:41

The disciples must have realised the tension in Jerusalem, they
must have known their Master was in danger, but they were so
very tired, physically and emotionally and they fell asleep. They
put themselves first whilst Jesus stayed awake praying in agony,
putting Himself last and murmuring, 'Thy will be done'. Lord, I
pray for staying-power . . . show me that if I fall asleep then I
leave the opportunity open for the powers of evil to take over.
Help me to stay spiritually wide awake however physically tired I
may be . . . Lord, please forgive my weak body and my half-
hearted intentions – I want to say the spirit is willing and the flesh
too, is willing.

Weak is the effort of my heart,
And cold my warmest thought;
But when I see Thee as Thou art,
I'll praise Thee as I ought.

John Newton

7th November

We have this hope as an anchor for the soul, firm
and secure:

Hebrews 6:19

In Paul's graphic description of the shipwreck just off Malta, he wrote of the danger of being dashed on the rocks so the crew threw four anchors over the stern of the ship – and prayed! Their anchors had gone . . . they were at the mercy of the waves and of their God. Shipwrecks come to all of us at some time or another, moments when we feel we are going to be dashed against life's cruel rocks. Our hope lies in not throwing away our anchor . . . in the most testing and traumatic situations we need to cling harder than ever to our faith . . . the anchor of our soul. Lord, in strained relationships, in unpleasant discoveries, at times when things are beyond my control I will pray that I will never lose my anchor . . . my hope.

> *Now I have found the ground wherein*
> *Sure my soul's anchor may remain;*
> *This anchor shall my soul sustain*
> *When earth's foundations melt away.*

Johann Rothe

8th November

Jesus said: 'You have heard it said, "Love your neighbour and hate your enemies," but I tell you, love your enemies and pray for those who persecute you.'

Matthew 5:43

Lord, it's against all my instincts to feel pleasant towards enemies, let alone care for them. And Your words make me realise how far away I am from fully understanding Your Gospel. Help me to learn a largeness of heart from those who have experienced the mental, physical and spiritual hell of war, and this day, as the world honours valour and remembers tragedy, I will nurture compassion for people from all nations whose hopes, dreams, bodies and loved ones have been destroyed by enemies.

O Lord, remember not only the men of good will, but also the men of ill will. But do not remember all the suffering they have inflicted on us, remember the fruits we have gathered, thanks to this suffering – our comradeship, our loyalty, our humility, the courage, generosity, the greatness of heart which has grown out of this: and when they come to judgement, let all the fruits which we have borne be their forgiveness.

from a prayer found in a concentration camp
written on a tiny scrap of paper

9th November

Jesus said: 'God is Spirit and his worshippers must
worship Him in spirit and in truth.'

John 4:24

In medieval times sheep browsed in London's West End where the church of St Martin in the Fields still stands as it has stood for centuries, looking out over poverty and progress. The Staff at St Martins worship God in spirit and also the truth by their active caring for those caught in the downward spiral of life – those whose entire possessions fit into a plastic bag. Lord, thank You for the witness of this place and for all the others like it, that more may be led to worship not only with their lips, but with hearts and hands as well.

Our social work is not just something attached to the church but an expression of the worship itself.

Austen Williams

10th November

The word became flesh and lived for a while among us.

John 1:14

The greatest mystery of all time – God descending to earth, to live in the form of a human man . . . the Almighty reduced to my level of experience — growing up, hard work, bruises, friendships, deaths; Jesus knew all these things. Lord, sometimes when I read the Bible, the language gets so involved and I just don't understand theological phrases, I don't really know what their deepest meaning is. Does it matter? I grasp the fact that Jesus was the Son of God — that He lived, He died and in resurrected power He lives forever. Lord, I believe these things and that I can have a fuller, more meaningful life because of Him.

There are three kinds of 'word': spoken, written and lived. The spoken word cannot be touched or denied but it makes an impact and is real. The written word cannot be retracted and has to be used with utmost care. The word lived is human personality. The bible is all three in the person of Jesus Christ.

Ian Thomson

11th November

> He was pierced for our transgressions, He was crushed for our iniquities, the punishment that brought us peace was upon Him and by His wounds we are healed.

Isaiah 53:5

A desperately sick prisoner of war was caught in the act of stealing a banana in a Japanese prison camp — he was sentenced to be flogged, but the padre, knowing that the prisoner would never live through a flogging, begged to take the man's place. The Japanese captors thought this amusing and happily went along with the substitution, making the prisoner stand by to watch as the padre was beaten for the crime he had not committed. Through the action of the padre the prisoner experienced the meaning of a hymn he remembered from Sunday school days . . . that act of self-sacrifice brought him to the foot of the cross to accept Jesus as his Lord and Saviour. Easter is a long way away now, Lord, don't let me drift away from the realisation of what You did, what You suffered . . . for us, for me.

Bearing shame and scoffing rude,
In my place condemned He stood:
Sealed my pardon with His blood
Alleluia! What a Saviour!

Philipp Bliss

12th November

Jesus replied: 'No man who puts his hand to the plough and looks back is fit for service in the kingdom of God.'

Luke 9:62

When the trees are bare and hedges have been cut back, newly ploughed fields stand out in the winter sunshine like giant patches of brown corduroy draped over the countryside. The harvest has gone and the whole cycle begins again, preparing the earth with the plough. The furrows are so even and consistent because the tractor doesn't stop and start every so often – the ploughman begins and carries on taking a pride in the uniform furrows. Lord, I pray that my preparations for things could be as even and consistent – I seem to be stopping and starting, hesitating . . . help me to put time and effort into preparations whether they be for a coffee morning or Bible study . . . show me that You demand only my best.

We plough the fields with tractors
With drills we sow the land
But growth is still the wondrous gift
Of God's Almighty hand.

Christian Aid words

13th November

Once more I will shake not only the earth but also the heavens . . . that is, created things, so that what cannot be shaken may remain.

Hebrews 12:26

Discoveries over the centuries have shaken the very foundation of science and belief from finding out that the world is round to extracting teeth with anaesthetic. Wars have torn people and countries apart and political shake-ups occur with such regularity nobody raises an eyebrow . . . our world has leapt forward in the span of a lifetime from horse-drawn carriages to supersonic flight. Dear Lord, what progress, what unimaginable change . . . what lies ahead? Today, I worship a God who is constant in this ever changing world . . . when my faith is shaken, Jesus be my Rock . . . when friends shake me and values seem to fall apart, Lord, be my foundation.

> *Christ is made the sure foundation . . .*
> *Binding all the church in one.*
>
> Anon: Late 7th. century

14th November

> Though outwardly we are wasting away, yet inwardly we are being renewed day by day. . . . So we fix our eyes not on what is seen but what is unseen, for what is seen is temporary, but what is unseen is eternal.
>
> *2 Corinthians 4:16/18*

All the words I read and sing, Lord, proclaim Your glory, Your Almighty and everlasting power and then I go and behave as though that were the last thing I believed. Unimportant things loom into great problems and before I know it the day is revolving around me. I am in danger of losing my awe and wonder — in danger of spiritual decay . . . lift my eyes, Lord, to values which are not just for five minutes but Your values which are eternal; by conscious effort may I draw close to You that my life may be renewed each day.

God does not die on the day we cease to believe in a personal deity, but we die on the day when our lives cease to be illumined by the steady radiance, renewed daily, of a wonder, the source of which is beyond all reason.

Dag Hammarskjold

15th November

Keep yourselves in God's love as you wait for the
mercy of our Lord Jesus Christ to bring you eternal
life.

Jude 21

We all look for heroes – the ideal example from a man or woman
on whom we can model our lives and with whom we can identify.
Two people worthy of being looked up to and followed are
Leonard Cheshire and his wife Sue (Ryder). Over the past forty
years and more the way they have lived their lives for others
because of their deep faith, has given thousands a glimpse of
God's love. O Lord, give me Your strength for today to live with
others for You and to live with You for others.

*Grant peace and eternal rest to all the departed, but especially to
the millions known and unknown who died as prisoners in many
lands, victims of the hatred and cruelty of man. May the example
of their suffering and courage draw us closer to Thee through
Thine own agony and passion and thus strengthen us in our desire
to serve Thee in the sick, the unwanted and the dying, wherever
we may find them. Give us the Grace so to spend ourselves for
those who are still alive, that we may prove most truly that we
have not forgotten those who died.*

Leonard and Sue Cheshire

16th November

Then a cloud appeared and enveloped them, then a
voice came from the cloud – 'This is My Son whom
I love, Listen to Him.'

Mark 9:7

Nothing is so totally disorientating as fog – suddenly we can't
recognise places, we don't know where we are or where we are
heading; it's frightening, frustrating and it reduces us to dithering.
Lord, I know Life can't always be sunshine and plain sailing, so
when the 'clouds' come down help me to know Your presence and

guiding hand just as surely as in the 'sunshine' . . . I will perhaps listen more attentively to Your voice in the fog of difficulty, whatever happens, Lord, I cannot see tomorrow, therefore I will trust You perfectly for today.

I was once a passenger aboard a ship that was being guided by radar. The fog was so dense we couldn't see the water about us. But the radar screen showed a streak of light indicating the presence of another ship far ahead. The radar penetrated the fog — so also is faith the radar that sees reality through the clouds.

Corrie ten Boom

17th November

Be very careful then, how you live . . . making the
most of every opportunity.

Ephesians 5:15

On the whole we tend to live each stage of our lives rather carelessly and then end up with too many regrets. We can never recapture our youth again nor can we ever recapture the words we ought not to have said . . . they have gone for ever just like our lost opportunities. Lord, help me not to get depressed by silly things like the weather — if I am bored and listless give me the humility to see that it is my fault and the common sense to go and do something about it. Forgive me if I end up tonight with regrets — I pray for Your guidance to make me more careful tomorrow.

Teach me Thy patience; still with Thee
In closer, dearer company,
In work that keeps faith sweet and strong,
In trust that triumphs over wrong;
In hope that sends a shining ray
Far down the future's broadening way
In peace that only Thou canst give,
With Thee, O Master, let me live. . . .

Washington Gladden

18th November

Trust in the Lord with all your heart and lean not
on your own understanding.

Proverbs 3:5

There aren't many weeks of this year left now, and when I look
back over what has happened I must confess that I have not been
100% trusting . . . I have found it difficult to be confident in
Paul's words, 'everything works together for good for those that
love God'. Lord, I have relied on my own judgement, my own
resources, and when they have run out I have given up. Your
promises are stacked high if only I would learn them – believe
them; when my heart is in turmoil, hold me in case I lose heart,
draw me closer to lean on You.

*If God has promised to guide His people (and He has), then if you
sincerely want to do His will, He does guide you, even when it
doesn't seem like it.*

Cliff Richard

19th November

The word of God is living and active.

Hebrews 4:12

It's no use looking back to the days when people flocked to
churches in this country . . . we must look at times and people
objectively. Years ago, the only social life in a village or town
centred on the churches – the only affordable social life for the
mass of folks, and, there was nothing else to do. People were not
committed – if anything the reverse is true. Today, if a person goes
to worship, it is because they really want to do so – there are
plenty of other things to do. Lord, thank You for the example of
committed Christians who prove that the Good News of Jesus
Christ, Your living word, is active and working right now, in
towns, cities and villages.

Lord, Thy word abideth
And our footsteps guideth;
Who its truth believeth
Light and joy receiveth.

Henry W. Baker

20th November

Wherever the spirit would go, they would go, and
the wheels would rise along with them, because the
spirit of the living creatures was in the wheels.

Ezekiel 1:20

Where would we be without wheels? The car for work . . . the
school bus . . . the milk float . . . the coal lorry . . . petrol tanker,
hospital cars . . . the list is endless. All these wheels working away
and we only notice them when we start complaining that the bus is
late or some other hiccup annoys us and puts our schedule out.
Today I want to give thanks for all this transport unknown to past
generations – Lord, progress is very wonderful at times; may the
words of Thora Hird challenge me as I focus my attention on
wheels.

Is faith your steering wheel – or only your spare wheel?

Thora Hird

21st November

All those men were under the supervision of their
fathers for the music of the temple of the Lord.

1 Chronicles 25:6

I think it's fair to say more people are moved by music than by any
amount of words: it touches the emotions and for a few moments
we are lifted beyond ourselves into the joy of worship. Music
enables us to 'feel'. Today is the anniversary of the death in 1695
of the famous musician Henry Purcell – a genius, who though
only 37 when he died, spent his talent for the Lord. Thank You

Lord for the wide range of music which gives me happiness, tranquillity, music by which I can join with others to worship and music which makes me feel better and more alive in my faith.

Celebrate the eternal God with harp and psaltery,
Timbrels soft and cymbals loud
In His praise agree.
Praise Him every tuneful string:
All the reach of heavenly art
All the powers of music bring
The music of the heart.

Charles Wesley

22nd November

Jesus declared: 'I am the bread of life. He who comes to me will never to hungry. . . .'

John 6:35

A loaf of bread – one of the oldest foods in the world, a staple basic food, not very exciting but necessary. Bread may be very old in one sense but when we buy it, we want it to be fresh each day. In John's first letter he states that he is not writing to the new Christians a new command, but a very old one, yet the life, death and resurrection of Jesus transformed the old commandment into a new one . . . fresh every day, the basic requirement for our spiritual nourishment. Lord, this is yet another fresh day . . . I come in prayer seeking the bread of Life.

Here, Lord, we take the broken bread,
And drink the wine, believing
That by Your life our souls are fed,
Your parting gifts receiving.

Charles Venn Pilcher

23rd November

Jesus said: 'unless an ear of wheat falls to the
ground and dies, it remains only a single seed'.

John 12:24

One way of looking at this phrase is to realise that it is useless for
us to stand alone, we must mix and we must at times bury our
self-centredness. The farmers know the only hope for harvest lies
in sowing seed . . . burying the grain to bring new life from the
ground to shoot and multiply. Too many of us resist letting go of
the world, we hold on to our selfish desires refusing to hear the
words of Jesus that we must 'lose our lives to save our souls'.
Lord, lead me to greater understanding of Your message – take
away my diffidence at making the step of commitment.

> *Until the seed is planted*
> *It cannot multiply;*
> *Nor can we see rich fruitage*
> *Until to self we die.*

Anon

24th November

For the wages of sin is death.

Romans 6:23

We are a society attuned to being paid for our effort, salaries,
wages . . . payment for a job. Likewise, the Bible tells, we shall be
'paid' for our sins, the misuse of our time, the dismal eroding of
our Christian principles . . . the lies, the jealousy, the theft of
another's property or partner. Lord, the road downhill is so easy,
forgive me for the way I have drifted away, stupidly wallowing in
the consequences of my sin; I would look again at the Lamb of
God who died to save me from the inevitable reward of my sinful
nature. My behaviour does not deserve Love . . . I ought to be
overwhelmed by such a Holy Sacrifice, the ultimate, wonderful
gift.

Look not on our misusings of Thy grace,
Our prayer so languid and our faith so dim;
For Lo! Between our sins and their reward
We set the passion of Thy Son, our Lord.

William Bright

25th November

. . . but the gift of God is eternal life in Jesus Christ
our Lord.

Romans 6:23

Yesterday, I thought about the consequence of sin but today I would dwell on the end of the verse – the alternative. God's gift of eternal life. Not a wage, nothing I've earned, but a gift of pure love. How hurt I should be if I offered a wedding present to a couple and they ignored it, leaving me to take it home again. To my shame, that is how I have treated the gift of love; Lord, I need Your love so much, flood my life with the light of Your presence and through Jesus Christ may that gift be mine.

For God so loved the world that He gave His only son, that whoever believes in Him shall not perish but have eternal life.

John 3:16

26th November

Unless the Lord builds the house its builders labour
in vain.

Psalm 127:1

The desperately poor and war-ravaged African country of Chad would not be the 'world's' idea of the most suitable place for a young Swedish couple to live, work and bring up their four children. Yet KeA and Birgitta Arnlund worked for Mission Aviation Fellowship – the organisation which gives wings to God's word in developing countries. The daily task of using small planes to transport food, building materials, agriculturalists, nurses and ferrying sick to hospital brings a working miracle into the lives of the needy. M.A.F. have pilots and Christian workers in twenty-two countries and all these committed men and women are there to build a better existence for their family in Christ. Today Lord, I pray for this brave and caring ministry in Your name.

I am more and more convinced that in whatever work we are involved, the Lord has to be the motivator and the driving force in our lives. We can have very fine organisations and high humanitarian goals, yet not be letting the Lord accomplish His work in our lives. I would encourage everyone to make themselves available for the fulfilling of the Lord's purposes in their lives.

KeA Arnlund

27th November

And being found in appearance like a man he
humbled himself and became obedient to death –
even death on a cross.

Philippians 2:8

Humility is not something we can pretend – it is sincere acceptance of our unworthiness before God, to be willing to learn God's will with the openness of the children put in front of Jesus. John Bunyan learned the hard way that there is no room for Pride in the Kingdom of God as he languished in prison. He suffered because he would not promise to give up preaching the gospel – he humbled himself, submitted his will before his Heavenly Father and was obedient to his unshakeable belief and through his ordeal the Holy Spirit upheld him and inspired the book Pilgrim's Progress. Lord, I pray for a meek, humble and sincere attitude.

He that is down needs fear no fall
He that is low, no pride,
He that is humble, ever shall
Have God to be his guide.

John Bunyan

28th November

'My prayer is not for them alone. I pray also for
those who will believe in me through their message,
that all of them may be one.'

John 17:20

So Jesus prayed not only for His immediate disciples but for all
future disciples – and that means even me. And He prayed for our
unity . . . oh, how far removed is today's picture of global Christianity with hundreds of sects and divisions. Lord, I want to learn
how to turn to You naturally, just as Your Son, Jesus prayed
freely, I ask that my prayers may be so frequent and so natural
that they become an integral part of my day. I would pray for the
little old lady who has gone into hospital, for the young couple
about to get married, for the widow facing retirement; for all
those I know who need the support of prayer, I bring their needs,
and mine, to the throne of Grace.

*At first we communicate with God through words. However, the
silent prayer which has moved beyond words must always spring
from everyday life, for everyday life is the raw material of prayer.*
Michel Quoist

29th November

Give us today our daily bread. . . .

Matthew 6:11

To be a mother of four young children is a full-time claim on a
woman's life but when one of those four has Downes syndrome, it
can create many and severe pressures within the home. Ann is a
former Sunday School pupil, and now a Sunday School teacher of
many years, she is dedicated and her home is a place of love and
welcome. She is self-effacing about how she copes with her family
except to say that she does not plan ahead but she tries to live one
day at a time and she finds the Lord gives her strength for each
day. O Lord, I am humbled by how families cope with enormous
problems, they remain cheerful and faithful – challenge me to do
just a little more for others with my life.

Lord, for my sake,
Teach me to take
One day at a time.

Marijohn Wilkin &
Kris Kristofferson.

30th November

Be still and know that I am God.

Psalm 46:10

Christmas is coming and I'm about at the end of my tether! So much preparation towards Christmas . . . so much to do and not enough time, not enough money . . . I could almost wish Christmas wasn't coming at all. Let me close my eyes, Lord, shut out the clamour of jingling bells and fat Father Christmases . . . I need to be quiet . . . to be still. How foolish I have been rushing and tearing around letting the secular and material side of the Christmas jamboree take the upper hand – in this moment of stillness I can see only one thing matters: there is a God, He cares for me and great will be my celebration of praise for His Son's birth.

Only be still,
And wait His leisure in cheerful hope:
With heart content to take what'ere Thy Father's
Pleasure and all-discerning love has sent.

Georg Neumark

1st December

How beautiful on the mountains are the feet of
those who bring good news.

Isaiah 52:7

Bad news may travel like lightning, but it is good news which people want to hear. The Jews longed for good news amidst their national woes, their dreams of the Day of the Lord and the reign of God as King of all the earth dominated their thinking and buoyed them up in darkest hours. In our Christian belief that Jesus the Messiah has come to the world, we can sing the good news that our God does, indeed reign. Lord, reign in my heart today and give my feet the urgency of good news.

How lovely on the mountains are the feet of him
Who brings good news, good news;
Proclaiming peace, announcing news of happiness —
Our God reigns, our God reigns.

L. E. Smith Jnr

2nd December

But you Bethlehem Ephrathah . . . out of you will come for me one who will be ruler over Israel.

Micah 5:2

In Advent we trace the longing and the prophesies for a Messiah; the nationalistic hope the Jews for a just ruler, a redeemer and King to destroy all their enemies still echoes in the world's need for peace and justice. Country after country hides repression, corruption, violence, double standards — the time is right once more to look to Bethlehem, but not merely in hope of what might be, but in the certain knowledge of what great life came from Bethlehem and will rule in our hearts today and always. Lord God, in Your spirit bring peace to my life . . . rule over my home.

Born Thy people to deliver;
Born a child and yet a King;
Born to reign in us for ever
Now Thy gracious kingdom bring.
By Thine own eternal spirit
Rule in all our hearts today.

Charles Wesley

3rd December

The light shines in the darkness, but the darkness
has not understood it.

John 1:5

The one book in all the world of which everyone has heard – or
nearly everyone – is the Bible; the Holy Scriptures . . . the inspired
word of the Living Lord. A revolutionary Book – a life-changer
. . . a challenge to all who pick it up. Today I think of all the
translators of the Bible and those who produce the Bible in braille;
I give thanks for the courage of those who take Bibles to countries
whose governments are hostile to the Gospel. I pray for any today
who will pick up the Bible for the first time, Lord, may they find
Your word an unfailing light for the rest of their lives.

*O God, we thank Thee on this day for the sacred scriptures, for
the comfort the Bible has brought to the sorrowful, for guidance
to the uncertain . . . we thank Thee most of all that it reveals to us
Thy son. Help us to ponder . . . that Thy word may indeed be a
lamp unto our feet and a light unto our path.*

Leslie Weatherhead

4th December

Remember the Sabbath day by keeping it holy. Six
days you shall labour and do all your work, but the
seventh day is a Sabbath to the Lord your God.

Exodus 20:8

Plenty have to work on a Sunday nowadays, we expect firemen,
policemen, ambulancemen, doctors, nurses, motorway service
station staff and so on to be on call but there is great physical value
as well as spiritual value in a day given to the Lord. That is not to
say, no-one smiles, no-one chops wood or washes up . . . it is
making the Lord important within our lives, our routine, our
work – making that special effort to make Sunday different by
praise and worship – giving God the glory. I'm thinking about this
now, Lord, on a Friday, praying that You will guide me how best
to make my Sunday 'holy'.

Christianity recognises no distinction between prayer and action . . . God 'works without ceasing', died working on the cross . . . Praying is no excuse for not working, and work is no excuse for not praying.

Louis Evely

5th December

For God does speak . . . though man may not per-
ceive it . . . a man may be chastened on a bed of
pain.

Job 33:14/19

The old Jewish idea of ill-health or ill-fortune generally, being a punishment is very deep-rooted. When pain and illness hit us we tend to feel cheated, the 'what have we done to deserve this?' syndrome. O Lord give me the ability to look beyond the frailty of myself to Your eternal purpose . . . instead of being depressed and having negative thoughts, I pray to learn from pain that whatever I have to suffer it is nothing compared to the suffering of Jesus on the cross. In the cross of Christ I glory.

Through pain and trials the Lord impressed upon my heart that He had kept me for His service. So now, for more than 50 years I've been telling others through my singing, witnessing and the printed page that Christ can save, bless and use people for His glory.

Henry G. Bosch

6th December

My hand will sustain him; surely my arm will
strengthen him.

Psalm 89:21

About a hundred years ago, Dr. Jeremiah Rankin was minister of a congregational church on the east coast of America. On Sunday evenings he would lead Bible study then encourage the congregation to sing lively (for those days!) and popular music. The people loved to sing the new and 'goey' hmns and Dr. Rankin himself wrote one as a Christian goodbye. This hymn has lodged itself in hearts on both sides of the Atlantic and indeed all round the world. Lord, I pray today for those I long to be close to but are thousands of miles away . . . in Your love may we feel united.

> *God be with you till we meet again*
> *When life's perils thick confound you;*
> *Put His arms unfailing round you,*
> *God be with you till we meet again.*
>
> Jeremiah Rankin

7th December

For to us a child is born, a son is given.

Isaiah 9:6

Birth is always a tremendous time of joy . . . unlimited speculation as to what the child will do in life and discussion as to which side of the family he or she takes after. Mary, that lowly and loving young mother must have sat nursing Jesus wondering what he would be like in manhood; did she ever dream her infant would change the world, that from the birth of her son history would be altered . . . He, the baby in her arms was the Holy Promise made flesh and blood. Lord, help me to approach the celebration of Christ's birth with renewed hope for the world.

> *Hail to the Lord's anointed,*
> *Great David's greater son;*
> *Hail in the time appointed,*
> *His reign on earth begun —*
> *He comes to break oppression, to set the captive free;*
> *To take away transgression and rule in equity.*
>
> James Montgomery

8th December

Such things must happen, but the end is still to come. There will be earthquakes in various places, and famines.

Mark 13:8

Man is so clever, so powerful and yet the earth's crust only has to move a matter of inches and the upheaval is so colossal and the fearful power unleashed in seconds so devastating, that all our cleverness is useless. The power needed for the creation of this planet cannot be measured let alone understood: just think – my Lord is the God of Creation, the power of my life . . . He is all powerful and I am nothing, yet I believe that same power comes to me in the inner consciousness of my heart. Lord, I pray to hear that still, clear voice speaking through the noise, destruction and upheaval of my world.

After the wind there was an earthquake, but the Lord was not in the earthquake. . . .

1 Kings 19:11/12

9th December

Do not forget to entertain strangers, for by so doing some people have entertained angels without knowing it.

Hebrews 13:2

Lord, You know there are people that I'm delighted to welcome into my home but there are others whose approach makes my heart sink – I don't want to be unfriendly, but my welcome varies enormously. I know it's wrong of me and I know too that around the Lord's table there is a welcome for everyone . . . so who am I to pick and choose! Lord, I pray for the eyes of Jesus to look on people, for the patience of Jesus in dealing with people and for the warmth of His love to encompass all strangers.

In memory of the Saviour's love
We keep the sacred feast;
Where, every humble, contrite heart
Is made a welcome guest.

Thomas Cotterill

10th December

There is a time for everything:

Ecclesiastes 3:1

Many of us live by the clock: a time to set the alarm, a time for the train, a time to go to the dentist, a time the play starts or a time for hospital visiting. Each activity of the day is allotted its time and place — but our God is not contracted to 'time' as we know and understand it, He is the God who was, who is and who is to be . . . a living, relevant God of all times and all seasons. Lord, forgive me when I say that 'I haven't got time . . . ' it's a funny thing that I've always got time to do what I want to do. Help me today to live using my time to the best of my capabilities . . . teach me to give time to people, time especially for prayer; there is a time for everything if I want to find the time.

Time like an ever-rolling stream bears all its sons away;
They fly forgotten, as a dream dies at the opening day.
O God our help in ages past, Our hope for years to come;
Be Thou our guard while troubles last
And our eternal home.

Isaac Watts

11th December

Charm is deceptive and beauty fleeting, but a
woman who fears the Lord is to be praised.

Proverbs 31:30

The Beauty Market is a multi-million pound bonanza . . . everyone wants to look good because in advertising terms beautiful is popular and successful. Yet however glossy the packaging or persuasive the slogan, one thing is very sure – physical beauty does not last. But there is a radiant beauty which is enhanced through experience and whose continuing influence is more far-reaching than any advert – that is the beauty of a woman who walks closely with her Lord. A woman who is gentle, soft-spoken, encouraging and caring will draw others to her. Thank You, Lord for those in my life who have left the indelible touch of Your love.

> *Let the beauty of Jesus be seen in me*
> *All His wondrous compassion and purity,*
> *Oh, Thou Spirit Divine,*
> *All my nature refine*
> *Till the beauty of Jesus be seen in me.*
>
> Albert Orsborn

12th December

This is the message we have heard. . . .

1 John 1:5

Eighty-six years ago today Marconi received the first ever trans-atlantic message from Cornwall to Newfoundland. People didn't believe for a moment that it could be done! It was a miracle! Yet, such a modest forerunner of the transistor radio, satellite T.V., the numerous other discoveries like micro-chips and lasers. Who would have guessed the progress that would be seen in this one century alone in the field of communication? The world has been made smaller, less frightening, foreigners less strange – it is Your world, Lord, help me to spread a message of love.

> *Take my lips and let them be*
> *Filled with messages from Thee.*
>
> Frances Ridley Havergal

13th December

And Saul's son Jonathan went to David and helped
him to find strength in the Lord.

1 Samuel 23:16

It's nice to have lots of friends but when we are in need we don't
want lots of people, we look for the special friend. Jonathan and
David had that special relationship where faith and love are
shared, where there is comfortable understanding without words.
It is interesting to note that although David was the Lord's an-
ointed, he was the one feeling in the dumps and it was through
his friend's loyalty and help that he turned to the Lord to find
strength – David needed Jonathan. Today, Lord, I pray for my
friends and give thanks for all the ways they help me and bring me
to see a clearer view of living uncluttered by self. I need them . . .
and I need the strength of my Lord.

> *I've found a Friend, O such a Friend*
> *So kind, and true and tender!*
> *So wise a Counsellor and Guide*
> *So mighty a Defender;*
> *From Him who loves me now so well*
> *What power my soul shall sever?*
> *Shall life or death? shall earth or hell?*
> *No – I am His for ever.*

James Grindlay Small

14th December

'You will be with child and give birth to a son and
you are to give him the name, Jesus.'

Luke 1:31

For a few frantic weeks the baby Jesus will be depicted on Christmas cards, portrayed by a doll in countless nativities, we shall sing
about the baby Jesus in the carols and generally enjoy ourselves.
Lord, I don't want to fall into the trap of worshipping a pretty
picture . . . a sweet, romanticised figment of Victorian imagina-

tion; the baby born to be King of all the World was born in poor and squalid surroundings . . . times were hard, human life was cheap. Help me to remember that He was given a special name, Jesus, Emmanuel – meaning God with us, and may I live to the glory of His name.

> *Jesus, name above all names, Beautiful Saviour,*
> *Glorious Lord, Emmanuel, God is with us,*
> *Blessed Redeemer, Living Word.*

N. Heard

15th December

Here I am. I stand at the door and knock.
Revelations 3:20

Our highways and byways are full of signs: Halt! Stop! Keep Out! Private, No Entry . . . we are very good at keeping vehicles and crowds in their rightful place but, sadly, sometimes there is a danger of our hearts and minds being similarly signposted. We may have been hurt, so we erect a high hedge around the heart saying 'Keep Out!' We secretly grudge giving so much time to church work so we nail a little notice in our mind saying 'Stop!' or there may be things we enjoy which are not compatible with Christian living, so we hang a notice on that part of our life saying, 'Private'. Lord, if I have done any of these things, forgive me. There is no part of my life that I want to keep You from . . . I pray that You will come into my heart – today.

> *'Tis the Saviour who would claim entrance to your heart,*
> *Will you send your Lord away?*
> *'Tis your Saviour, 'tis your Saviour standing there,*
> *Haste, and let Him in! let Him in!*

J. Pollard

16th December

He will judge between many peoples and will settle disputes . . . nation will not take up sword against nation, nor will they train for war any more.

Micah 4:3

What a wonderful vision the prophet Micah had of a world at peace under the rule of the Lord. To look back in history, it seems that every nation has spent most of its time, energies and resources in war . . . all the valiant young lives in every century, lost in the fields of hate and desolation. Lord, I look around this world preparing for Christmas – preparing to sing loudly 'Hail the heaven-born Prince of Peace' and I see countries torn by civil war, dragged down economically and morally – I pray for the innocent civilians, women and children who suffer today and I join my prayers with theirs, for peace.

Nation with nation, land with land,
Inarmed shall live as comrades free;
In every heart and brain shall throb
The pulse of one fraternity.

John Symonds

17th December

We have this treasure in jars of clay to show that this all surpassing power is from God and not us. . . .

2 Corinthians 4:7

I take for granted my standard of living – I take it as my right, my well-deserved and just reward . . . if I think at all, it is to feel I ought to have more. I conveniently forget that nothing in this world lasts forever; food decays, money depreciates, cars rust, clothes fall out of fashion, even my body begins to give out and not operate with the same smooth co-ordination as it did twenty years ago. The only lasting treasure I have is the gift of redeeming love. Lord, help me to give true appreciation to my 'present', to laugh and have fun in simple moments, for they are all passing and will never return. . . . Make me realise that I am nothing, but my life has purpose if infused with Your Holy Spirit's power.

For Thine is the Kingdom, the power and the glory. For ever and ever, Amen.

The Lord's Prayer

18th December

Joseph went to Bethlehem to register with Mary
who was pledged to be married to him and was
expecting a child.

Luke 2:5

Lord, I remember the first time I touched the velvet softness of a baby's head – counted perfect little fingers – tickled tiny toes . . . such utter helplessness yet Your saving love is predestined for each life. Take me in faith to the manger, to gaze on the Christ-child – vulnerable to all man's evil yet born to overcome evil with goodness. Lord, I praise You for the birth of Mary's boy . . . the hope of the world and the Light of my life.

Clear shining light, Mary's child,
Your face lights up our way;
Light of the world, Mary's child,
Dawn on our darkened day.

Geoffrey Ainger

19th December

Great crowds came to Jesus, bringing the lame, the
blind, the crippled, the dumb and many others, and
they laid them at His feet.

Matthew 15:30

Through all the jolly tinsel, the parties, the carol-singing and the over-eating, my mind goes out to those who face physical pain and discomfort this Christmas time . . . those who live unable to see the lights and decorations, those who sit in wheelchairs, the children who cannot communicate – I bring those I know to the feet of Jesus in prayer. Lord, give me Your compassion and let me learn from their courage.

There is, in fact, no better cure for self-pity than Lourdes. Where the sick and the maimed to pour together to proclaim their hope and their faith, or even just to share their fears, it is no longer possible to believe that one's own pain is either unique or unbearable.

Mary Craig

20th December

Awake! Awake!

Isaiah 51:9

Excitement mounts! I do love to hear the carols and the special Christmas music – then there is that annual miracle of pleasantness in the High Street, that intangible warmth when perfect strangers are not embarrassed to smile and exchange seasonal greetings. Decorations are up, lights twinkling on the Christmas trees and all the smells of Christmas cooking in the air. Yes, Lord, I must wake up before it's too late, before this time of holy joy has melted into January . . . I must wake up and play my part in making this Christmas celebration the most meaningful ever.

Wake O wake with tidings thrilling,
The watchmen all the air are filling
Arise, Jerusalem, arise . . .
Go forth and join the festal throng.

Philipip Nicolai

21st December

There is hope for your future.

Jeremiah 31:17

The world scene is frightening – millions of war-heads, the capacity to destroy the whole planet several times over, the threat of nuclear war – all too appalling to think about, but God says there is hope. In her book, 'Blessings', Mary Craig writes about a Polish couple; he had been in Auschwitz, she in Ravensbrück. After the war the wife died and the husband, Stefan, wrote about his children 'They are in God's hands – I hope they will learn to have compassion for others'. Out of the experience of the concentration camps, God had given Stefan the ability to hope . . . even when his wife died. Today, Lord, I put my trust in You and place my hope in the future because of Jesus, my Saviour.

> *All my hope on God is founded;*
> *Me through change and chance He guideth,*
> *Only good and only true:*
> *Christ doth call, one and all*
> *Ye who follow shall not fall.*

based on Joachin Neander

22nd December

A day of darkness and gloom, a day of clouds and
blackness.

Joel 2:2

The shortest day . . . getting to the depths of winter now; dark, gloomy mornings and early evening blackness. Lord, the gloom tends to get inside me, I feel another year is slipping by, and I've wasted so much time, so much I hoped to do has just not happened . . . I feel colourless and flat. You understand my glooms and dooms, Lord, Help me to understand that just as the earth needs time to rest and recover, so I need a bit of rest too. Give me grace, to rest, together with the assurance that these days of gloom will not last for ever, before I know it the days will be lengthening once more.

> *Shine through the gloom and point me to the skies:*
> Henry Francis Lyte

23rd December

> A shoot will come up from the stump of Jesse . . .
> the Spirit of the Lord will rest on him –
>
> *Isaiah 11:1*

Jesse was the father of King David who was born at Bethlehem, a town some six miles south of Jerusalem. The gospel writers of Matthew's and Luke's gospel give long genealogical records to prove that Jesus was born a direct descendant of David. Jesus, Himself knew the prophesy and quoted from Isaiah chapter 61 when He preached: 'The Spirit of the Lord is upon me . . . ' Lord, it will make the celebration of Christ's birth more important if I can grasp the longing felt by the Jews for their Messiah . . . I need to be able to understand that and also to realise that the majority of people today, though ready to enjoy a festivity, are quite unaffected by the Messiah.

> *Thou art the King of Israel,*
> *Thou David's royal son;*
> *Who in the Lord's name cometh*
> *Thou King and blessed one.*
>
> Theodulf of Orleans

24th December

> Glory to God in the highest. And on earth peace to
> man. . . .
>
> *Luke 2:14*

The singing of the angels in heaven at the birth of Jesus has echoed

across the centuries and this year it seems as though carols have
been sung for weeks. Now the mad, material rush is almost over,
the spiritual journey through Advent has reached the climax. I
wait . . . mystically joined with the family of God across the
world . . . praying, hushed, expectant –
God bless Your world tonight –
God bless my family and friends –
God bless me.

The wireless brings us songs of Christmas praise,
*   From far and near;*
And listening, we are one with you today
*   Friends . . . everywhere!*

Yamamoto
Japanese Christian leper

25th December

Today, in the town of David a Saviour has been
born to you: He is Christ the Lord.

Luke 2:11

Today we commemorate the birth which changed history.
Nothing else like it has happened before or since, nothing so
unites the world, this joy – even if it doesn't last, people really do
act differently at Christmas. As I read, sing and listen to the story
of the birth in that long ago stable, I pray for my faith to be born
again, in simplicity, in humility, in the child-like trust which
unlocks the key to the kingdom of God. Lord, I come to the town
of David, to Bethlehem . . . I come to the infant Jesus – please . . .
come to me.

O holy child of Bethlehem descend to us, we pray,
Cast out our sin and enter in, be born in us today.
We hear the Christmas angels the great glad tidings tell;
O come to us, abide with us, our Lord, Immanuel.

Phillips Brooks

26th December

The shepherds said one to another: 'Let us go to
Bethlehem and see. . . . '

Luke 2:15

Somebody once said 'God must be very fond of ordinary people
for He made so many of us!' In His ministry, Jesus was accused of
mixing with all types, tax-collectors, publicans and prostitutes
. . . His closest friends were fishermen and the first visitors at His
manger were shepherds. Jesus worked as a carpenter, using His
skill for farmers and builders. Lord, I'm ordinary – I don't even
have a present to offer the new-born King, but I will join with the
shepherds, traffic wardens, shop assistants, postmen, train-
drivers, teachers – I will join with people everywhere in the eager
press to turn again to the stable and worship. Kneeling there, I
could offer my heart. . . .

Shepherds in the field abiding
Watching o'er your flocks by night:
God with man is now residing: Yonder shines the infant light;
Come and worship – Come and worship
Worship Christ the new-born King.

James Montgomery

27th December

Where is the one who has been born King of the
Jews?

Matthew 2:2

No-one will ever know precisely who the three strangers were
who sought the King of the Jews. They may have been Kings, Wise
Men, Ambassadors – speculation is interesting but useless. Whoever they were they had gone to a great deal of trouble, expense
and exposed themselves to personal danger, so their goal must
have been more precious to them than life. Lord, the story is so
familiar I no longer look for meaning in it . . . today, I ask myself
where is the one who has been born? Is He at the back of my mind

already . . . or have I put Him at the centre of my life? Is He going to be worth trouble, expense or danger to me or will I let Him stay tidily on a Christmas card until next year.

> Eastern sages at His cradle
> Make oblations rich and rare:
> See them live in deep devotion
> Gold and frankincense and myrrh.
> Sacred gifts of mystic meaning
> Incense doth their God disclose.
> Gold the King of Kings proclaimeth
> Myrrh His sepulchre foreshows.
> Prudentius 348–410 A.D. tr. E. Caswall and others

28th December

> . . . and they returned to their country by another
> route. . . .
>> Matthew 2:12

Christmases can be predictable – even 'samey', same kind of food, same games, same carols, same services, same people . . . there can be a faint air of anti-climax after the event, it wasn't quite how we had hoped. Lord, I don't want my faith to become routine and stagnant; after a vision of Holy Innocence coming into the world, I don't want to get straight back in the same old rut . . . I want to return to the world from the manger by another way. Lord, I ask for courage to venture from the safe and predictable round of post-Christmas activities – show me a new way of keeping alive the joy of Christ's birth.

> Onward, ever onward, journeying o'er the road,
> . . . journeying on to God:
> Leaving all behind us may we hasten on –
> Backwards never looking, till the prize is won.
>> Godfrey Thring

29th December

Simeon took Him in his arms and praised God
saying: ' . . . my eyes have seen Your salvation.'

Luke 2:28

We read that the spirit of God was upon the old man Simeon, and because he was waiting the spirit led him to see the Light of the World. There must have been so many distractions in the temple yet Simeon was led to one special couple; Lord, help me to see reality through all the distractions of my day and because I believe that no earthly, evil darkness will overpower the Light of Life in Jesus Christ, I will live contentedly.

> *Lord now let thy servant depart in peace,*
> *For Your word has been fulfilled;*
> *My own eyes have seen the salvation which You have*
> *Prepared in the sight of all people:*
> *A light to reveal You to the nations,*
> *And the glory of Your people Israel.*

Luke 2:29–32

30th December

An angel of the Lord appeared to Joseph in a
dream . . . 'take the child and His mother and
escape to Egypt. Stay there until I tell you, for
Herod is going to search for the child to kill him.'

Matthew 2:13

Rage and blind jealousy goaded Herod in this dispicable act of butchery. He was determined at any cost to eliminate any threat to his own power and prestige. The world is in a similar state today, there are many who seek still to stamp out the Prince of Peace . . . in the name of justice terrible acts of torture are committed, in the name of peace, war-heads and nerve gases are hoarded, in the name of religion men and women distrust and hate each other. Lord, what a mess! I pray for those who are blinded by jealousy and hate, whose hearts are so evil. . . . The Jewish leaders thought they had killed You two thousand years ago – give me confidence that Your reign of Peace and Justice will begin, it will come and never ever be overthrown.

Herod then with fear was filled:
'A Prince,' he said, 'in Jewry.'
All the little boys he killed
At Bethlehem in his fury.

15th century tr. Percy Dearmer

31st December

They will not need the light of a lamp or the light of
the sun, for the Lord God will give the light.

Revelation 22:5

One whole year . . . gone! I'm a year older so I ought to be a year wiser but it doesn't seem to work out like that. If I had known everything that was going to happen over the past 365 days I couldn't have coped – thank You, Lord for being my strength. I pray that what I have learnt may help someone else – at least I have more sympathy. Now, as I face the unfolding of the brand new year, I give You my hand, Lord – I praise You for all that is past and trust You for all that's to come.

And I said to the man who stood at the gate of the year: 'Give me a light that I may tread safely into the unknown.' And he replied: 'Go out into the darkness and put thine hand into the Hand of God. That shall be to thee better than a light and safer than a known way.'

M. L. Haskins